C000194043

"One thing I h
Valley—I am not the onl
every other person I
reavement, or sufferin
rapport, we can commu........., ...p....

"One has lost a dear one years ago and the wounds remain. . . . Another exists daily with but a step between life and death. Some can tell of alcoholics in the family, constant turmoil, frayed nerves, sleepless nights, mental anguish. I never dreamed so many were in the dark Valley. . . . We have joined the fraternity of the broken-hearted, veterans of warfare with the powers of darkness, some are shell-shocked from the conflict, never to be quite the same again. We read in the Bible of a great multitude who have come out of great tribulation. . . .

"Our Lord is the Leader of this society. He was a Man of Sorrows and acquainted with our grief. . . . Nobody ever walked through so dark a Valley and He walked it by Himself. . . . He has been through the Valley and we need fear no evil for He walks it with us.

"So cheer up, my fellow traveler, wending your way through dangers, toils, and snares you will meet a host of kindred souls. . . . And, best of all, as with the Hebrew children in the fiery furnace, there is Someone else in the fire; you are in the company of the supreme Sufferer who drank the bitter cup to the dregs. . . .

"He has long since made it home through the dark Valley. And so shall we."

Though I Walk
through the Valley

Also by Vance Havner

The beloved Southern Baptist preacher Vance H. Havner is known as one of the greatest revivalists of the twentieth century. Born in Jugtown, North Carolina, he began writing sermons for the local newspaper at age nine, was licensed to preach at twelve, and was ordained as a minister at fifteen. A preacher for more than seventy years, he is the author of over thirty books.

Though I Walk through the Valley

Vance H. Havner

SPIRE

Published by Fleming H. Revell
a division of Baker Book House Company
P.O. Box 6287, Grand Rapids, MI 49516-6287

Spire edition published 2000

Second printing, November 2000

Printed in the United States of America

ISBN 0-8007-8665-3

Unless otherwise indicated, Scripture quotations are from the King James Version of
the Bible.

Scripture quotations identified PHILLIPS are from The New Testament in Modern
English, translated by J. B. Phillips, copyright J. B. Phillips, 1958. Used by permission
of Macmillan Company.

For current information about all releases from Baker Book House, visit our web site:
http://www.bakerbooks.com

CONTENTS

Preface

Ever since I started writing books in 1934 I have covered many notes in the scale from the comic to the tragic. I have sought to rebuke and reprove and exhort and also to comfort and cheer. But now grief and sorrow and bereavement have been my bedfellows and what I once knew only by observation I know now by experience. Only those who have traveled this road really know what the journey is like. I am not building up a theory in these pages or marshaling the well-worn clichés. This is a record of months of watching my dearest die. The fears and disappointments alternate with seasons when hope rose high and prayers seemed about to be answered. I have not revised it but have left the whole story with its ups and downs day-by-day. It is my prayer that this account may bolster the faltering faith of some fellow traveler who, like myself, walks through the Valley—and that trip lies ahead for all of us, sooner or later. Never forget, it is a walk THROUGH the Valley and it is the Valley of death's SHADOW. We are not driving down our tent pegs in these lowlands for there are heights beyond!

VANCE HAVNER

Though I Walk
through the Valley

1

The Walk Begins

1973 began with promise. Sara and I had a fine schedule of meetings planned until spring and early summer. Then we meant to take a much-needed vacation, part of it in our beloved mountains and especially along the Blue Ridge Parkway at a little lodge we often visited. Everything started off well enough with two weeks in Florida, other meetings in Baton Rouge and Richmond.

Then the roof fell in. Sara had a virus attack in Fayetteville, North Carolina, and her symptoms worsened. I went on to Nashville and she to the doctor who immediately assigned her to intensive care in the hospital. Her trouble was first diagnosed as diabetes but soon changed to a malady I had never heard of and about which the doctors do not know enough—Cushing's Disease. If Sara had checked the list of all available ailments she could not have picked one more obscure and strange. An endocrinologist might tell you that certain glands produced an excess of hormones that threw her body balance out of order. Her face and legs were swollen, her features were distorted until she did not look like herself, she could not walk. For two weeks her mind lapsed into confusion, she could only stare and talk incoherently. There were personality changes and she was not herself. I sat for weeks looking at her disfigured features unable to communicate with any satisfaction.

All disease originated with the entrance of sin into this world but some illnesses bear more of the marks of that origin than others. Cushing's Disease is not an old, well-known trouble we can chart through a long and familiar history. There is something weird, uncanny, queer about it that suggests almost demonic ingenuity. We are contending with the powers of darkness and spiritual agents from the very headquarters of evil. This attack on one so sweet and gracious who had been so healthy did not classify it merely as another run-of-the-mill disease in the book but an assault of the Enemy to cripple our ministry. Satan comes as a roaring lion, as an angel of light, as an accuser of the saints. Clearly this was a tempestuous onslaught just as the devil attacked Job within the permissive will of God. It is well to recognize and not underestimate our Adversary and we are not to be ignorant of his devices. Our Lord spoke of the afflicted woman "whom Satan hath bound" (see Luke 13:16) and Paul identified his thorn in the flesh as "the messenger of Satan" (see 2 Corinthions 12:7). Some maladies bear peculiar marks of the wiles of the Enemy and we do well to add a Scriptural diagnosis to whatever any clinical tests might reveal.

So began my journey through the Valley. The beloved Twenty-Third Psalm calls it the Valley of the shadow of death. The Valley may not always mean death but at least we walk in its shadow. That is a long shadow when it lengthens into months. I was assured that although I walked through that Valley I need fear no evil for the Shepherd's rod and staff would comfort me. I remembered that my Lord said in His darkest hour, "Now is my soul troubled and what shall I say?" and then He prayed, "Father, glorify Thy Name" (*see* John 12:27, 28). When we do not know what say, we DO know what to say: "Father, glorify Thy Name." I made it my prayer and so began my walk through the Valley.

The Valley of the SHADOW of death. When one faces the light, the shadow is behind him. When we face heavenward our shadows are behind us. And with us is the Light of the World!

2

Considering the Circumstances

I write this during some of the darkest days of all my nearly seventy-two years. For weeks I have sat in a hospital beside my dear wife who is ill with a strange malady from which there seems to be poor medical hope for recovery. Sitting for weeks in a hospital is enough to make a well man sick. All our plans are in shambles and we face an array of problems to which we

have no answer. One might say with Jacob, ". . . all these things
are against me" (Genesis 42:36).

I took a stroll below the hospital along the edge of the woods.
The woods always refresh a tired soul. As best I could I
reaffirmed the blessed promise: "Commit thy way unto the
Lord; trust also in him; and he shall bring it to pass" (Psalms
37:5). That three-part recipe begins with a definite act of
commitment. Then the step of faith is followed by the walk
of faith, ". . . trust also in him . . ." and it ends with victory,
". . . he shall bring it to pass."

We are so often creatures and victims of circumstance. Ask
someone, "How do you feel?" and you may get the answer,
"I'm doing the best I can UNDER THE CIRCUM-
STANCES." Our Lord said, "In the world ye shall have tribulation [pressure]" and when has there ever been so much pressure as now! "but be of good cheer; I have overcome the
world"(John 16:33). Our Lord lived and died under the darkest
of circumstances. He was under the constant pressure of the
powers of darkness. The world, the flesh, and the devil were set
against Him and they finally nailed Him to a cross. But He
overcame the whole combination and lives forevermore!

The Christian does not have any business living UNDER
the circumstances. He can live ABOVE them, reign in life,
taste the powers of the age to come, live in kingdom come in
his heart while he makes his way through an evil and hostile
world. He looks not at things seen but at things unseen. He is
MORE than conqueror. He does not merely triumph, he tran-
scends.

Nor must he fight his way THROUGH circumstances. No

amount of flexing our muscles and gritting our teeth and furiously battling the fog will do it. We mount up with wings as eagles above the tempest instead of exhausting ourselves wrestling with it.

You can go crazy considering the circumstances. Plenty of people have. You can live a life of fear, worry, defeat UNDER the circumstances. You can exhaust yourself trying to battle THROUGH the circumstances. Jesus came to defeat the devil, the world, and death. He lives in every Christian's heart and we have victory because He is the Victor. The Holy Spirit came to make all this real and operative and we have built-in power that no circumstances can defeat.

I do not write this on a sunny day when everything is in good shape and conditions are most favorable. I write it on a dark day when circumstances are the worst I have ever faced. So cheer up, my troubled reader, this is not a little pep talk by somebody with not a trouble in the world. Such people often try to sympathize, but you have to go through this to know what it is like. This is a testimony born of adversity. I am considering Him who endured contradiction of sinners in the worst of circumstances, lest I be weary and faint in my mind. I am not UNDER the circumstances, my life is hid with Christ in God. In that fair realm I am ABOVE all circumstances this world can devise. One day that fair realm will be my eternal abode where dear ones do not suffer or depart, hearts do not break, tears are wiped away, and circumstances cannot reach us—for the former things (circumstances!) will have passed forever away.

3
"Trusting Jesus, That Is All"

Our Lord had much to say about taking no anxious thought for our lives, food, drink, or raiment. He spoke of the birds and the lilies as examples of God's care. He said, ". . . be ye [not] of doubtful mind" (Luke 12:29). He told us that the Gentiles worry about such things and, since Christians belong to another race and nation as children of God, we should not worry as they do about such matters. Paul wrote, "Be careful for nothing . . ."(Philippians 4:6).

When we doubt or fear or worry we are not believing. Christ lives within us and He never worries. Faith is the opposite of fuming and fussing. All doubt is sin for it denies God's Word. Hannah Whitall Smith pointed out that if "According to your faith be it unto you" (Matthew 9:29) is true then conversely, "According to your doubt be it unto you" is true also. It takes some of us a long time to stop trying and begin trusting. Some never do. The greatest adventure in this life is to quit merely reading it, talking about it, praying about it, and reach that point where we can actually sing:

> Simply trusting every day,
> Trusting through a stormy way;
> Even when my faith is small,
> Trusting Jesus, that is all.
>
> E. PAGE

There is no moment of any day when it cannot be done. It will not be easy, for feelings and circumstances will laugh at us. It may seem utterly unreal, especially at first, and all the powers of darkness will team up against anybody who dares to really walk by faith and not by sight. We become automatically the targets of the devil. But faith grows as we exercise it, and old thought and life patterns of the natural man fade as the new man puts on the Lord Jesus Christ and lets Christ live in him.

Our Lord said, "Consider the lilies, how they grow" (Luke 12:27). They do not work and strain and fuss about it, they just grow. The birds neither sow nor reap or gather into barns but God feeds them. This does not mean we sit around and wait for God to send in the groceries. We must sow and reap and gather into barns but we are not to worry about it. Not a sparrow falls without our Father's notice. They do fall, mind you, but they don't sit around fretting about what day they will fall. Children do not lie awake at night worrying about whether their parents will feed and clothe them. Insomniacs worry all day over whether or not they will sleep at night. One might as well worry over whether we will be hungry at mealtime. We try to help nature out but when we are normal the laws of God need no help. Our Lord said we must be converted and child-like to enter the kingdom. He made a happy, trusting child His model.

Start today to "let go and let God." Cast all your cares upon Him for He cares for you. "Commit thy way unto the Lord; trust also in him; and he shall bring it to pass." Any moment of day or night, the adventure is on! Say no to all doubt and unbelief for they are of the devil and we must slam the door

in their face and not entertain them for one moment. The
mustard seed will move the mountain if we do not doubt.
Wisdom will be given but we must not waver.

This is the victory that overcomes the world when we are
shipwrecked on God and stranded on Omnipotence! It is not
a fad but a fact. This is IT, the very essence, Christ in us the
hope of glory, our lives hid with Christ in God.

4
A Kentucky Meditation

I am writing this in Kentucky where I am speaking at an
assembly. It is hot July and I am alone, for Sara is an invalid
at home. I was to have stayed in a motel where we were put
up a year ago but they moved me and I am glad, for it is much
harder to stay alone in such spots after we have been there
together. It has been a lonely trip but I am not alone. The day
before I started, God gave me in my *Daily Light* a promise for
these days: "My grace is sufficient for thee for my strength is
made perfect in weakness" (2 Corinthians 12:9). And Paul
added, ". . . when I am weak, then am I strong"(12:10). I found
myself saying, "Lord, You have the strength and I have the
weakness—let's team up!"

One of the speakers on the program this week lost his wife five years ago. *(Lost* is not the right word for Christians divided by death. You haven't lost anything when you know where it is!) He has never gotten over his bereavement. His fellowship has been a blessing. In times like these, many dear souls with the best of intentions try to console us. Many speak from observation but few from experience. You have to go through it to know what it's like! The dear brother says the verses God gave him when his wife died were 1 Corinthians 2:9,10: "But as it is written, Eye hath not seen, nor ear heard, neither have entered into the heart of man, the things which God hath prepared for them that love him." And then the blessed word, "But God hath revealed them unto us by his spirit. . . ." These things God has prepared refer not only to joys awaiting us in heaven but blessings available NOW. We can have a foretaste of glory and of the powers of the age to come. We can sample the fruit of the land before we reach the heavenly fields or walk the golden streets. If such advance blessings are to be had we ought to lay hold upon them now! The promises of God are not mere mottoes to hang on the wall, but checks to be cashed —and if we ever needed them we do now! If there is a bank account in our name we ought to use our checkbook of faith and prayer. While we lay up treasure in heaven we may also draw funds to our credit and heavenly cash for our earthly needs today.

These days find me living in the strength of Another. My own resources are exhausted. I am like the poor fellow who said, "I've wrecked my constitution and am living on my bylaws."

My doctor said to me when I started this trip, "You'll just

have to do the best you can." But if I did the best I could I wouldn't last a week! I want to do the best that Christ can do in me and for me and through me, exceedingly abundant above all I can ask or think. The little pin I carry in my wallet says, "To me to live is Christ." I want to make that pin not a rabbit's foot or a talisman, but a reminder of a glorious reality.

> Lord Jesus, make Thyself to me
> A living, bright reality;
> More present to faith's vision keen
> Than any outward object seen.
>
> ANONYMOUS

It is not fancy, it is fact. I have transferred my cares to Him and He has taken over. This does not reduce me to an automaton, a robot. I have a will and when it is merged with God's will I have merged with the Almighty, shipwrecked on God and stranded on Omnipotence—and what a good place to be stranded!

5
Living as Though

I write this in the stillness of a summer sundown in the lovely lodge of Pine Mountain Park in Kentucky. My back porch opens to a matchless view and the evening sun sinks low behind a nearby mountain. A robin sings just outside and as a special favor a wood thrush chimes his vespers like his forbears used to do when I was a boy on the farm.

The one dearest to me lies gravely ill. Our doctor, almost as concerned for me as for her, told me not to return for a few days, remembering my eleven weeks vigil by her hospital bed. I am torn between being there and being here—watching with her and preaching in this preacher's school for a few days.

Down through these years I have marvelled at how when the load is heaviest and my frame the weakest, God brings me to a spot made to order for the hour. If ever there was an ideal place for a respite from some of my darkest days, this is it. All my days I have been aware of One going before me and with me, of doors ajar that I never could have opened.

> Can I doubt His tender mercy,
> Who thro' life has been my Guide?
>   FANNY J. CROSBY

I do not know just why after thirty-three years of happy comradeship with the dearest of companions there should crash upon us this weird and uncanny disaster, but I know that God sends no test heavier than we can bear and provides with that test a way of escape. So I will not despise His chastening nor faint when I am rebuked of Him. As He reminded Peter in another connection, what He does I know not now but I shall know afterward.

My verse in *Daily Light* today says, "Wherefore criest thou unto me? speak unto the children of Israel, that they go forward" (Exodus 14:15). Would my Lord have me stop begging for personal favors, groaning in my distress, and get busy preaching to His people, His church, with new fervor? God shuts His prophets up to Himself when He would make them His spokesmen. Our Master laid down terms of discipleship so drastic that we have been trying to water them down ever since. ". . . let the dead bury their dead" (Matthew 8:22). Those who would proclaim His Kingdom have no time to be undertakers and mourners at the graves of this world. Akin to this is the stern word about hating loved ones and one's own life for His sake. We have toned down this stern word to a mild relativism, so weak that it disturbs us not at all. To be sure, it does not mean despising life and loved ones. Most of us do not love our dear ones enough! But in escaping one extreme we have gone to the other and the verse has lost its flaming challenge.

Again one thinks of 1 Corinthians 7:29–31, about living "AS THOUGH." It does not say we are not to have wives or weep or rejoice or buy or use this world, but to live AS THOUGH we did not. It is about time we stopped watering down our

Lord's severe terms, His insistence on detachment in spirit if not in letter from all earthly concerns. We have reduced these to mere instances of glorified exaggeration, overstating a truth in order to drive it home. The result is a band of run-of-the-mill disciples who make little impact on this age because we are as they are. Our Lord lost many a prospect because He would not mark down the price of utter devotion. We fill our churches with these dime-a-dozen Christians who hear the Word and with joy receive it but crumble under persecution. We shall make poor progress until we can rally a persecuted minority, scorning the values of this world and living by stringent discipline.

6
Is Thy God Able?

When Dr. Blank had his nervous breakdown a specialist advised him to stop preaching, shut up his study, put away his books, and get his mind off religion. When Mrs. Doe suffered similar exhaustion the expert told her to give up church interests, join a club, go to the movies, and change her mind completely. Along the same line was the counsel given by one preacher to a very conscientious fellow minister: "You ought to smoke a big cigar and learn to cuss a little."

We freely grant that one can become too absorbed in religious matters and may need to balance these with other interests. Certainly getting outdoors, fishing, golf, a new hobby, a change of scenery, all these have therapeutic value and aid in restoring body, mind, and spirit. But turning to worldly pursuits, to the theatre instead of church, replacing devotions with dancing, having a fling to offset too much serious living, this is the counsel of men and not of God and I do not buy it.

If a man cannot turn to God in the hour of his deepest need and come boldly to the throne of grace for help in such a time, then the gospel means nothing and Christian experience is a delusion. I do not find David seeking relief from his troubles in some ungodly diversion. He had tried one foray into sex that scarred his soul forever. Our Lord set no example of turning to the world in the hour of trial. He said, "In the world ye shall have tribulation [pressure]: but be of good cheer; I have overcome the world." The New Testament does not advocate relaxing one's conduct to let the hair down when in distress. There should be healthy and happy enjoyment of life's innocent pleasures indeed, but we need not call in Satan under the guise of a specialist or renounce our holy walk because our nerves have failed. The Twenty-Third Psalm has comforted more distraught, sick souls than all the clever tricks offered by the world, the flesh, and the devil.

Our God is a very present help in trouble and just when we need Him Jesus is near. I remember one bleak evening during these weeks of testing when I came into a lonely motel room where I was to stay while I preached for a few days. The Bible lay open on the table at Psalms 42 and this precious verse:

> Why art thou cast down, O my soul? and why art thou disquieted in me? hope thou in God: for I shall yet praise him for the help of his countenance.

Call that coincidence if you will but I call it Providence!

When Jeremiah and Micah saw conditions at their lowest ebb and the outlook was bleakest they saw the way out: "Thou, O Lord, remainest forever" (Lamentations 5:19); "Therefore I will look unto the Lord" (Micah 7:7). And when worst comes to worst we can say with Jehoshaphat, ". . . we [know not] what to do: but our eyes are upon thee" (2 Chronicles 20:12). Our God is not a fair-weather friend. He is accessible and available in the darkest hour. We need not turn to this world where all around us we see change and decay. We can pray with confidence, "O Thou who changest not, abide with me."

Darius asked Daniel in the lion's den, "Is thy God . . . able to deliver thee from the lions?" (Daniel 6:27). If He is not able in life's darkest hour, He is not able, period. The Hebrew children said, "Our God . . . is able to deliver us from the burning fiery furnace . . ." (Daniel 4:17). He was and He still is!

7
Comrades of the Valley

One thing I have learned in my journey through the Valley —I am not the only one who has traveled this trail. Every day I meet some fellow pilgrim. Almost every other person I talk with has been scarred by tragedy, bereavement, suffering. They open up to me for they know how it is. If you have never been there yourself, you don't know how it is. You cannot share by imagination or observation. You have been there or you haven't. If you have been there, then we have rapport, we can communicate, we speak the same language.

One has lost a dear one years ago and the wounds remain. Another lives with a companion whose life hangs by a thread from day-to-day. Another exists daily with but a step between life and death. Some can tell of alcoholics in the family, constant turmoil, frayed nerves, sleepless nights, mental anguish. I never dreamed so many were in the dark Valley, but misery loves company and makes us partners. We have joined the fraternity of the brokenhearted, veterans of warfare with the powers of darkness, some are shell-shocked from the conflict, never to be quite the same again. We read in the Bible of a great multitude who have come out of great tribulation. I have joined the society and their fellowship is precious because THEY KNOW. They do not speculate, philosophize, recite pet clichés. They do not make light of my troubles. Only fair-weather travelers who have known little sorrow do that.

Our Lord is the Leader of this society. He was a Man of Sorrows and acquainted with grief. He was tempted in all points as we are. Nobody ever walked through so dark a Valley and He walked it by Himself. We can never suffer as He suffered, die as He died. He has been through the Valley and we need fear no evil for He walks it with us.

So cheer up, my fellow traveler, wending your way through dangers, toils, and snares you will meet a host of kindred souls. You have joined the brotherhood at the price of heartache and tears. Only the initiated know the password. And, best of all, as with the Hebrew children in the fiery furnace, there is Someone else in the fire; you are in the company of the supreme Sufferer who drank the bitter cup to the dregs. Your grief is but a passing twinge compared to the agony of His soul.

When I preach about these things, I can see some faces light up among the congregation. The Spirit blows on the coals and they glow. Others merely look on uncomprehending. They do not know and there is no way to share with them. They have not been through the Valley.

The Valley is not endless, it will not stretch on forever. Ira D. Sankey, the great gospel singer, went blind in his later years. When a friend visited him, Sankey sat down at his organ and sang with that voice that had blessed so many:

> There'll be no dark valley when Jesus comes
> To gather His loved ones home.
>
> WILLIAM O. CUSHING

He has long since made it home through the dark Valley. And so shall we.

8

Divine Chastening or Devilish Attack?

When Christians go through great testings such as is my experience just now, they sometimes wonder, "Is this the chastening of the Lord or an attack of the devil?" It can be both. In the case of Job, God was dealing with His servant but so was the devil. Satan can go only as far as God lets him go but that can be a long way sometimes! Paul's thorn in the flesh was allowed of God in order to teach the great apostle the sufficiency of divine grace, but Paul called the thorn "the messenger of Satan."

I am convinced my experiences just now are God's will and I would not despise His chastening nor faint at His rebuke. That classic passage on divine chastening, Hebrews 12:5–11, begins with a quotation from Job and moves on to attest that such trials assure us that we are truly God's sons. I had been for many years relatively free from trouble, grief, and distress and sometimes I wondered that I had known so little of that adversity that indicates our sonship. I have no doubt now! I am moving through the "grievous" part of Hebrews 12:11 toward the "afterward" with its peaceable fruit of righteousness. Whatever comes, I accept it and believe that it will work for good as part of the "all things" of Romans 8:28.

But this can also be the attack of Satan for anyone who preaches what I have been proclaiming makes himself the target of the enemy. The devil attacks body, mind, and spirit and will take from us health, loved ones, possessions, anything to discourage us and divert us from our mission. He has succeeded at times and prophets have watered down their message, ministers have left their pulpits, and hard-pressed saints have temporarily lost their faith. But sometimes he has overstepped himself and suffering saints have added to their spiritual wealth with gold tried in the fire.

The Book of Job opens with the sons of God assembled in the divine presence and Satan among them. This raises questions we can never answer now and although there is drama in its setting, it shows that things happen in the courts of heaven that would explain many an earthly puzzle if we could attend one session of God's sons reporting to the Father—and the devil among them!

We do know that we wrestle not with flesh and blood but with spiritual forces in the heavenlies and that we are the prime object of demonic assault when we expose sin and call men to repentance. How the chastening of our Father and the onslaught of our Foe can be pieced together in the pattern of our lives is not our business. Ours is to accept what is of God and resist what is of the devil and pray all the while for wisdom to distinguish the one from the other. Whether God and the devil have discussed you as they did Job and whether Satan has Divine permission to put you through the wringer to test the reality of your faith, I do not know. I know that what brought Job through was the final divine confrontation that led to an ending brighter than ever the beginning had been. No story ever ended more happily-ever-after than the Book of Job. May it be so with you!

9
Billy Goat at Ben Lippen

This week finds me at dear Ben Lippen Bible Conference high in the mountains, a favored spot for forty years. I came here first when the original building was an old post office brought out of Asheville and rebuilt. Being a bachelor at that time I suggested that they put me in the room marked "Unclaimed Mail." Here some of the best friends I have in this world gather in the summer and just now I feel deeply the blessing of their presence and their prayers. I am never so aware of the sweetness of the tie that binds our hearts in Christian love as at such a time and place as this.

The director of the conference based the morning devotions at breakfast on the Twenty-Third Psalm. This morning I awoke a bit blue in my spirits. My dear Sara lies in the hospital again and we are trying to get her into a medical center under an endocrinologist who should know more about her strange malady. But there is a delay in securing a room. My loneliness seemed intensified while old fears and dreads and doubts assailed me from the devil's headquarters. This morning the devotional message reminded us that we are the Lord's sheep but some of us are more like billy goats—always "butting." "Yes, I know the Lord is my Shepherd BUT . . . I'm growing old and who is going to care for me? What if I get sick and my helpmeet cannot come to my aid?" The devotional speaker did not know that he had a prize-winning old billy goat right beside him at the table!

Right here our experience often breaks down. We accept the promises, we recite the verses, we roll all the clichés under our tongues, but when trouble comes we begin with our "Yes, buts." Instead of "The Lord is my Shepherd, I shall not want" we really mean, "The Lord is my Shepherd, BUT I am in want." David did not write the Twenty-Third Psalm in the serene pastoral scenes of his boyhood. We do not know just when he did write it but it was somewhere in his stormy life, perhaps when his own beloved Absalom had rebelled against him and everything had crashed around him. If the Lord is not our Shepherd at such times as that, then this psalm is only a pretty little piece of fair-weather poetry.

After the breakfast devotions I climbed to the mountaintop nearby to get my perspective in order again and the Lord, in keeping with David's psalm, restored my soul. Surely He who has brought me through nearly seventy-two years of dangers, toils, and snares will see that I finish the journey. Surely goodness and mercy shall follow me the rest of the way and I shall dwell in the house of the Lord forever. Lord, help me to be a lamb and not a billy goat!

P.S. We got Sara into the medical center. Billy Graham from his home nearby sent word that if we had not gotten her in yet he would send Sara and me to the Mayo Clinic in a jet with arrangements made at both ends of the line. Darkness brings out the stars and trouble brings out friends old and new and blessings never possible in sunnier times. There are fair-weather friends, but thank God for the ones who show up when the Valley is dismal and the sun doesn't shine.

One thing is certain—the Christian has no business being a billy goat when God calls him His lamb.

10

My Soul Has Found a Resting-Place

With my dear one immobilized, this septuagenarian preacher has been faced with no resting-place at home or abroad. It is impossible to go somewhere for a break. I was planning to do just that when the storm broke and since then the pressure has been stepped up, the furnace heated seven times hotter.

But God has an answer: "My presence shall go with thee and I will give thee rest" (Exodus 33:14). Did not our Lord bid us come to Him and find rest? And do we not enter into rest when we cease from our own labors and rest in His finished work? "There remaineth a rest to the people of God," not only in heaven but now. "Entered into rest" was not meant merely for an epitaph on a tombstone. We do not have to reach it by way of a graveyard. We can enter our Canaan rest now. They used to sing when I was a boy, "O come, won't you come with your poor broken heart, Jesus will give you rest." His yoke is easy and His burden is light.

"My presence shall go with thee, and I will give thee rest." The rest comes not only in the fact of His presence but in the feeling of it. There is the knowledge of His presence and the sense of His presence. I do not ask God to be with us in a church service. He is! Where two or three gather in His name, He is there. Why pray, "Lord, be with us"? But we may pray for an awareness, a consciousness that He is there, a sense so often lacking in our meetings.

Here is rest when all else fails. We can take a vacation within if not one without. You need not seek rest in the mountains or by the sea if you do not have it in your heart. You cannot get away from it all if you carry it all with you. Paul did not end his days basking in a village by the sea writing his memoirs. He was awaiting an executioner's axe but his heart was at rest. He carried a portable chapel within and there he withdrew to renew his strength. So did our Lord who had no place to lay His head. You too must find that retreat within for no earthly hideaway can give you rest without. Take your vacation all along and when your life is hid with Christ in God you learn in whatever state you are to be content, gloriously independent of time or place. As Madam Guyon put it:

> To me remains nor place nor time;
> My country is in every clime:
> I can be calm and free from care
> On any shore, since God is there.

Moses asked the Lord, ". . . wherein shall it be known here that I and thy people have found grace in thy sight? is it not in that thou goest with us? so shall we be separated, I and thy people, from all the people that are upon the face of the earth" (Exodus 33:16). The one thing that distinguishes the church from any other company on earth is the presence of God with His people. It is that which makes a church service different from any other and without it we meet without meaning.

> All is vain unless the Spirit
> Of the Holy One comes down.
> GEORGE ATKINS

And it is the conscious presence of God in the life that makes a Christian a different person set apart from all others. His Spirit goes with His people and He gives them rest.

11
The Saviour and the Storm

Three of the Gospels tell us the story of the storm on the Sea of Galilee, the frightened disciples, the sleeping Saviour, and the stilling of the tempest. At the end of a busy day the tired Master got into the little fishing boat (not a private yacht!) and fell asleep. I like the way Matthew 8:24 puts it: ". . . there arose a great tempest . . . but he was asleep." The ship was covered with the waves but why should the Master of wind and weather be disturbed? It was His Father's world and what woke Him up was not the fury of the storm but the frenzy of His panicky disciples. Why did they not say, "There is nothing to worry about. The Lord of all creation is taking a nap and we are safe"? Instead, they got their eyes on the storm instead of the Saviour.

The weather is always a convenient topic for conversation but the Christian attitude toward the weather is rather mixed. We say, "God runs the weather" and of course that is true for "He's got the whole world in His hands." But Satan has some leeway there and uses it as he did with the mighty wind that destroyed Job's sons, the storm on Galilee, and Euroclydon on Paul's voyage to Rome. There would be no tornadoes, floods, hurricanes if sin had not entered the world. There will be no such upheavals when Jesus reigns on a redeemed earth.

Storms are part of nature ruined by the Fall. There are other kinds of storms and all for the same reason. The Christian travels a tempestuous sea in this old world but Jesus is in the boat. AND SOMETIMES HE SEEMS TO BE ASLEEP! When Lazarus lay ill and a hurry call was sent to the Master we read He stayed two days where He was. There is the love that tarries. God takes His time. He may seem slow but is never late. We go into panic but no tempest disturbs His repose.

> Whether the wrath of the storm-tossed sea,
> Or demons, or men, or whatever it be,
> No water can swallow the ship where lies
> The Master of ocean and earth and skies;
> They all shall sweetly obey My will;
> Peace, be still! Peace, be still!
>
> MARY A. BAKER

We forget, like Peter on that same Sea of Galilee, and we see the boisterous wind and the boiling waves when we take our eyes off the Lord walking in the storm.

Are you in a storm? Is it failing health, financial distress, family trouble, depression of mind? Does the Lord seem asleep and you feel like crying, "Carest Thou not that we perish? Lord, do something!" (See Mark 4:37–39.)

We read, "There arose a great storm" and then, "he arose." He will rise to your need at the proper time. He rebuked His disciples for their little faith but He did not dismiss or disown them and say, "Go, I'll get a better team." He labored on patiently with them and made them the spearhead of His church. So many times in the Gospels He reproved them for their little faith—and how must He feel toward us today! They cried, "Lord, save us"—that was faith. "We perish"—that was doubt. We are reminded of the father of the demented boy who cried, "Lord, I believe; help thou my unbelief" (Mark 9:24). At least he took sides with his faith, not his doubt!

We read that there were "other little ships" on the Sea of Galilee when this storm arose. There are many little ships sore beset today. The storms will arise but He too will arise—and the Saviour is the Answer to the storm!

12
Any Day Is V-Day!

When we are passing through great trial and testing we are inclined to wait until the storm is over and the battle ended before we celebrate victory. We lift our weary and tear-dimmed eyes to some blessed day ahead or to heaven itself and sigh for ultimate deliverance. We plod along through gloomy days and desolate nights looking for light at the end of the tunnel. Today is just another dark chapter to be endured.

But to the Christian, V-Day can be today, no matter what the circumstances are. ". . . this is the victory that overcometh

the world, even our faith" (1 John 5:4). Our victory was won
at Calvary and the open grave. Our Waterloo is behind us and
we are engaged only in mopping-up operations! When the
battle is fiercest and no end seems in sight, if we have walked
by faith and triumphed over fear in spite of feelings and conditions, that is victory NOW and we need not wait to celebrate.

I am passing now through a time of great trial. I do not know
what the outcome will be. I do not know when clouds will lift
and the burden fall. I am not merely trying to hold out until
then. Today can be a triumph as great and maybe even greater
than when the storm abates and the battle ends. I stand in
Christ complete. The full and final realization of His triumph
has not yet come. We see not yet all things put under Him but
we see Jesus and in Him everything is as good as done. This
IS the victory! There is no doubt as to the outcome. Sin, death,
and the devil are still here, disease and disaster, heartbreak and
bereavement are with us but they are defeated foes and we
have but to wait a little while to see them all forever past.

The Christian belongs to a Kingdom of the heart, an invisi-
ble world at present, but one day it will be set up visibly right
here on earth. Meanwhile we taste even now the powers of that
age to come and enjoy foretastes of glory before the King
returns. To move through this world as a citizen of heaven is
victory now. Principalities and powers battle us fiercely but
greater is He that is in us than he that is in the world, and by
the shield of faith we can ward off the fiery darts of the Wicked
One. The outcome is sure, there is not a moment's doubt as
to how it will all come out. The devil is on the way out although
he may stir up quite a rumpus in his exit.

You can end this drab day with celebration if you live it by the faith of the Son of God. We do not have to wait until we see how it will turn out. It has already turned out! This is the marvelous truth of the gospel that we start from victory and work from it. The ultimate outcome merely climaxes what is guaranteed from the start.

You do not have to stand on Jordan's stormy banks and cast a wishful eye to a distant Canaan. We are in Beulah Land now. We can shout hallelujah over the potential until we wait for the actual. True, we do not live by feeling but if all things are working together for good there ought to be some happiness now!

Let us celebrate victory provided in the past, possible in the present, perfected in the future but victory anytime! This IS V-Day! Ours is the Victor and we follow in the train of His triumph. All things are ours already and we are Christ's and Christ is God's.

13

You Never Miss the Water
Till the Well Goes Dry

For years I have written about the journeyings of Sara and
myself and her innumerable ministries as wife, homemaker,
and companion. I have told her many times what she has
meant to me and am so glad that I never took her for granted.
I was aware to some degree of what I owed to her and knew
that I could never repay that debt with word or deed. I was
often frightened when I wondered what would happen to me
if I lost her. What would I do with no one to meet me when
I came home, to care for me if I fell ill? ". . . woe to him that
is alone when he falleth; for he hath not another to help him
up" (Ecclesiastes 4:10).

But no matter how you value these dear ones and seek to tell
them, the full force of what they meant never breaks until they
are no longer able to help. "You never miss the water till the
well goes dry." You never knew what you had until you no
longer have it. Of course if death removes them we are not to
spend the rest of our days sitting up with the corpse and
wallowing in past memories. We must, as it were, let the dead
bury the dead and forget the things behind us. We must face
the future for the rest of life must be lived. But from our sorrow
we can at least offer a word of counsel to the multitude of our

fellows whose sin may lie in taking things for granted. We take
our homes and loved ones as a matter of course. Health we
enjoy and scarcely give it a thought until, in a hospital, we
realize that we didn't know what we had. Sleep, for instance,
is a blessing we never count. We just go to bed and sleep but
if, as was my experience for some years, insomnia grips us and
we lie all night waiting for morning, when depression hangs our
harp on the willows, then we miss the water of the well gone
dry.

How we take this country of ours for granted! It might cure
us to try living in some other lands. The heritage of our fathers,
the legacy of America, to this we rarely give a thought. Ask the
returned POWs and they can tell you how you miss the water
when the well goes dry.

And the church! We neglect it, we criticize it, we wouldn't
live where there are no churches but how many live AS
THOUGH there were no churches!

The gospel becomes a matter of course. Cursed with the
familiarity that breeds contempt, the privilege of hearing it
means nothing. Jesus Christ, who He is and what He did, we
have heard it all our days and what makes a new convert shout
for joy in the aisles puts us to sleep in the pews.

Think of the water of life. One can wait too long to appreciate that, and when the day of grace is over that remorse will
be ours for all eternity. The rich man in hell never missed the
water until the well went dry. He begged not for one *drink* but
for one *drop* of water to cool his tongue *(see* Luke 16:19–31).
It is a fearful picture and this generation does not accept it but
remember that it was the Lord Jesus Himself who painted this

view of the future of the lost. And the Scripture makes it plain that for millions the well of salvation will no longer be available.

Be on your alert about taking things for granted. Don't wait to thank God and others for the water until the well has gone dry!

14
When God Is Silent

I read it on a desk motto in a preacher's study:

> I believe in the sun when it does not shine. I believe in God when He is silent. I know the sun is up there even on the darkest day. And when darkness veils Jesus' lovely face, I rest on His unchanging grace.

One thinks of the line in that precious hymn, "Spirit of God, Descend Upon My Heart" that says, "Teach me the patience of unanswered prayer."

There are mountaintop experiences in our journey through this world, those rare and lucid moments when God is consciously near and speaks to us as a man speaks to a friend. There are those ordinary days when we may not be thrillingly aware of His presence but neither do we doubt it. But there are also those strange times when things do not add up or make sense, when we seem to be forgotten, when the heavens are brass, when instead of happy answers to our petitions, an ironic spirit laughs at us and makes mockery of our feeble faith. We sit with Job and wait for an answer that seems never to come.

We had better learn the faith that believes anyway when God is silent. Our Lord drank the bitter dregs of despair when He cried, "My God, my God, why hast thou forsaken me?" *(See* Mark 15:34). But He was forsaken only for a moment and then came Resurrection day. Our highest faith is when we leave it to God to keep to Himself why these utterly unexplainable things happen to us never to be understood this side of heaven. "Farther along we'll know all about it" and "We'll understand it better by and by" may seem scant solace now, but it is the best we can do until we get home.

God promised Abraham progeny as numerous as the stars, but many years passed before Isaac was born and Sarah rebelled against the delay and took matters in her own hand. The result was Ishmael and the bitter results of that mistake still remain. The Israelites in Egypt had to wait long to see the salvation of the Lord. Nothing they could do would be enough for deliverance. The four hundred silent years between Malachi and Matthew must have seemed endless, but they ended with the coming of the Saviour. God may seem slow but is never late. Sometimes He says yes. Sometimes He says no. Sometimes He just does not say and we can only wait. I believe in the sun when it doesn't shine for I know that shine it will, eventually. I believe in God when He does not speak. He says, ". . . they shall not be ashamed that wait for me" (Isaiah 49:23).

The sun has outlasted all the clouds of all the centuries. God is not forever silent. When the answer comes, here or hereafter, it will repay all the torment of unanswered prayer. The wait will not be as long as it seems. "The strife will soon be o'er" says the old hymn, and in the joy of His answer we shall forget the agony of the delay.

15
At the Medical Center

I stood in the medical center today amidst a formidable array of medicos, medicine, and machines. What an astounding assortment of devices man has assembled for the cure of disease and the prolonging of life! With it he does indeed produce wonders but the curse of disease remains, and it may be that for one ailment we conquer several new ones come along. Even our wonder drugs raise problems of their own. Man will never by his scientific skill erase from earth the fruits of his transgression.

I stood amidst all the men, medicine, and machinery and found myself praying, "Lord, I am only a little country preacher amidst all this display of man's intelligence and skill, but I represent the other side of this picture—Christ, the greatest Physician of all who healed the sick instantly without any means or paraphernalia. All He needed to do was to touch and speak. He could walk the waves and still the storm by a word. In the age to come all our gigantic and costly equipment will be unnecessary. We will not need to spend billions to reach the moon but can be anywhere in the twinkle of an eye. Only by cumbersome devices can man now work any of the wonders that will be natural and simple in the Kingdom to come."

When Jesus was on the earth He gave us in His miracles examples of what He can do and even today there are occasional interventions when He moves in to heal when all other means have failed. He does not always heal, and along with Paul and Publius we must remember Trophimus left at Miletum sick. Many questions arise. How can we pray with faith if we are not certain it is God's will to answer in this case? But sometimes there is faith for healing either on the part of the one healed or others. ". . . perceiving that he had faith to be healed" (Acts 14:9); "And Jesus seeing their faith . . ."(Matthew 9:2). "And there is given to some the gift of healing" *(see* 1 Corinthians 12:9). While it may not please God to heal every time, we often have not because we ask not or do not ask in faith.

No one has perfect faith. There may be little faith with much doubt or great faith with little doubt and all shades and degrees of faith between. As much as a grain of mustard seed will move a mountain. The father of the demonized boy prayed, "Lord, I believe; help thou my unbelief." He did not say, "I doubt; help thou my faith." Take your stand with your faith, not your doubt, and God will help your doubts.

We live in a sophisticated, skeptical day when it is not easy to just trust Jesus as they did long ago. If we lament that we could believe, too, if He were here among us visibly, remember that He said, ". . . . blessed are they that have not seen and yet have believed" (John 20:29).

So the little country preacher stands in the medical center, and while he converses with the splendid doctors there he whispers a prayer to another Physician none the less real because to sight unseen. The doctors give a favorable report of improvement on the part of my dear one and I look past all the medical center here to the greatest Healer of them all—His touch has still its ancient power. While we may look to the physicians within their limits, I would not sin like Asa in not looking beyond all that man can do to God Himself. There is a greater healing center above for body, mind, and spirit. How we need to visit that clinic for examination, diagnosis, and treatment! The door is open and any may come without money and without price.

16
Some Unanswered Questions

The Scriptures leave many questions about the hereafter
unanswered. Do children grow up in heaven? What about the
saints with the Lord who do not yet have their resurrection
bodies? What is a spiritual body? And of course through the
ages bereaved hearts have asked, "Shall we know each other
over there?"

Of course it has been said many times that surely we shall
have as much sense there as we have here! The Sadducees
asked our Lord about the woman who had been married seven
times: whose wife would she be in the resurrection? He replied;
"Do ye not therefore err, because ye know not the scriptures,
neither the power of God"? (Mark 12:24). When we know not
God's Word nor His power we fall into all kinds of error. Error
is grounded in ignorance. Jesus went on to say that in the
resurrection we neither marry nor are given in marriage but are
as the angels. He was not covering the whole subject of our
status in the hereafter and we can read too much into or out
of these words. He simply said that angels do not marry and
in this respect we shall be like the angels, for earthly relation-
ships do not obtain in the hereafter.

This does not necessarily mean that we shall feel exactly the
same way toward everybody, a stranger or our dearest loved
one. I do not know how God will work it all out and I may be

speculating, but I cannot feel that I will react just the same when I see my mother or wife over there as to somebody I never saw before. I know that we shall have new bodies and that old emotions will have been displaced by a new personality appropriate to our heavenly life. But I cannot think that there will be one general uniformity of thought and feeling with no degrees of delight as we meet again those we have loved long since and lost awhile. Our Father will grant us fullest joy, and I am not going to let the problem of one woman with seven husbands spoil my anticipation when I walk the golden streets with the one I loved above all others on earth.

Nor do I think that all the residents of that fair city will have the same capacity for enjoyment. The Scriptures teach that some will be beaten with few stripes and some with many and some shall rule over five cities and some over ten. By the same token I cannot believe that heaven will mean no more to faithful saints who walked close to God on earth than to some poor disciple who barely got into heaven saved as by fire with his life gone up in smoke.

Just how the Father will do it I do not know, but my joy will not be less there than here and it will be intensified, not toned down to one unvarying pattern. Even this poor world abounds in color and variety and my eternal home will be no monolithic set-up. I still feel that the dearest here will be dearer there in a way I could never know in this world. But I approach it with no trepidation. My Father knows how to do it and five seconds after I arrive all my questions will have disappeared in ecstasy as I take up my abode in the house of the Lord forever.

17
He Giveth His Beloved Sleep

Forty years ago while preaching through Iowa one summer, I had my first bout with insomnia. I went to bed one night and never slept a wink. I repeated the performance next night. For two years I tried to carry on in my preaching beset by sleeplessness and despondency. I counted sheep, took exercises, read everything I could find on the subject. I learned that many of God's choicest servants had suffered from my affliction. Dr. Torrey tells how he obtained relief through the Holy Spirit. I prayed diligently but still I couldn't sleep. I remember a night on Lake Minnetonka in Minnesota when I lay awake all night and had to preach in First Baptist of Minneapolis next day. I awoke with what seemed like blacksmiths hammering on the top of my head. I sometimes held on to the pulpit while I preached. I did not take sedatives for I did not want to develop a habit. I remember Dr. Riley of Minneapolis telling how he suffered from insomnia at one time and got along by taking short naps when he could instead of sleeping all night.

There was no magic deliverance, but in 1940 I entered my present traveling ministry, the last thing anybody would have recommended for my ailment. Sleeping in a different bed every week, living in hotels, constantly readjusting to new food, climate, and other conditions is not exactly the way out for an insomniac but God had called me to this ministry and I started.

Then I met and married dear Sara, and the new affection and the new work gradually wrought the blessed change until I could sleep under almost any circumstances.

When I began my present walk through the Valley the old trouble showed up again at first. The dreadful loneliness on the road when I was out preaching, no letters from my dear one, and no one to come home to, my concern as to what I would do without her—these problems beset my nights early in this experience. I quoted promises and endeavored to roll my burden on the Lord but it would not stay where I rolled it. But God came to my rescue and now I can testify that during these weeks past, through the most trying part of this walk, I have been able to cast my cares on Him who cares for me and I find that He sustains me. I think of the old bishop who could not sleep. One night he read the promise, "Behold, he that keepeth Israel shall neither slumber nor sleep" (Psalms 121:4). He laid his Bible up and said, "Well, Lord, if You are sitting up with us there is no sense in my doing it. Good-night, Lord."

We cannot foolishly break the laws of health and expect God to save us from the consequences. But when we are caught in circumstances from which we cannot take a vacation, as I find myself now, then we can look to our Father for strength to carry on. I have no easy, glib magic recipes but I can witness to His garrison of angels keeping my heart and mind with the peace that passes understanding. He knows our frame and remembers that we are dust. There will always be enough of everything we need to do all God wants us to do as long as He wants us to do it. I believe that includes the sleep He gives to His beloved. *(See* Psalms 127:2.)

The bottle of tranquilizers my doctor prescribed lies unused these nights. They have their place. I have used some earlier and necessity may again arise for their assistance, for God provides medical helps too. But just now I rejoice in the sleep He promised.

18
Land of Unclouded Day

I will remember these months past for my walk through the Valley (and I am still walking), for the Watergate scandals, and for some of the strangest weather of any spring and summer. I know that "He that observeth the wind shall not sow; and he that regardeth the clouds shall not reap" (Ecclesiastes 11:4) but I am an incurable cloud-watcher. I love the sunshine and my spirits rise and fall with the weather. We are nearing fall now and I approach it with sadness. William Cullen Bryant has written wisely concerning autumn: "The melanchoy days are come, the saddest of the year. . . ."

I find myself singing that old song, "The Land Of Unclouded Day." I know the prophet said the clouds are the dust of God's feet (see Nahum 1:3), that He established the clouds above *(see* Proverbs 8:28), that He covereth the heaven with clouds *(see* Psalms 147:8). I know my Lord will come with clouds *(see* Revelation 1:7) but I like best David's reference to a morning without clouds *(see* 2 Samuel 23:4). When I can begin the day with not a cloud in sight I am at my best. I know that clouds are necessary in the present order of things for clouds mean rain, but I envision a day when, like night itself, they will disappear from the scene. I know that in every life some rain must fall and some days must be dark and dreary, but I long for that better world where we shall enjoy the sunshine of unbroken fellowship with our God.

Today was to be sunny according to the weatherman. I am glad I never went into the weather forecasting business! It started out brightly enough but then came the clouds and all day long we have lived under a gloomy canopy. I have seen few bright days this whole season. Even at best there has been a haze. It may be because of pollution which has become such a fixed part of our life these murky days—pollution of the air, of the mind, of the spirit, of government, of humanity everywhere. It may be part of the general setup of the last days before our Lord returns, a fitting meteorolgical accompaniment of what we find everywhere else. I do remember three cloudless days in Kentucky months ago when my spirits soared, but they were the exceptions that proved the rule.

Thank God, we can have the Light of the World within and sing, "There Is Sunshine in My Soul Today" even if it rains all week. Our Lord made His way through many a dark day of opposition and died with the skies turning black, but He arose and we commemorate the Resurrection with sunrise services for sunrise speaks of a new day. A fair-weather Christianity will never carry us through such times as these. We are not always on the bright side but we are on the right side and the right side will be the bright side ultimately but not always immediately. For the joy set before Him our Lord endured the cross, despising the shame. It gets darker before it gets brighter. We are not saved to be Pollyannas wearing rose-colored glasses, waving "Cheerio," and painting the clouds with sunshine. Our Lord was neither an optimist nor a pessimist but a Realist. He saw things as they were and as they would be. The picture was often dark and forbidding but beyond He saw a new age and John saw a city that needed no sun for it was forever day. That is the Land of Unclouded Day and it is not pie in the sky, it is God's final and eternal provision for His saints who may weep through many a dark day here but are bound for a world where not only darkness but even tears are passed away. John is my favorite weather prophet and I'll abide by his forecast.

19
As I Await the Outcome

Sara entered the hospital in early April. Her trouble was first diagnosed as diabetes and other complications but later changed to Cushing's Disease. For some weeks she suffered, then made an astonishing partial comeback. She did not wish to continue taking tests and wanted to come home. We arranged it and she stayed for a few weeks, then had a relapse. We finally got her into a medical center and she underwent surgery for removal of the adrenal glands. She somehow survived major surgery, shingles, a blood clot, and a threat of pneumonia. At this writing she has taken a turn for the better but with a long way to go. I can only marvel that she is still with us and thank God for the faintest hope. She has the best of care, excellent doctors and nurses, but the medical outlook is guarded and the possibility of complete recovery not too clear. Our eyes are on the Lord who may intervene when men, medicine, and machines have done their best.

I have no pet theories about faith healing. I know that God does not heal everyone every time else no one would ever die. I have felt that if Sara were fully restored it would be a miraculous testimony in these days when we do not expect God to break through but, like the scoffers of whom Peter wrote, we argue that ". . . all things continue as they were from the beginning of the creation" (2 Peter 3:4). We do not look for miracles but only the laws of cause and effect with no outside intervention from heaven. God still breaks through when it is His will. Every time a soul is saved you have a miracle. (I mean of course by "saved" a genuine new birth, not a mere "decision.") Every answered prayer is a miracle. Every true revival is God breaking through. Why should it seem a strange thing for the great Physician to hear and heal when all else has failed?

But, whatever happens, I realize that we can make one episode more important than the whole story, one act more important than the entire play. Our business as Christians is to glorify God, whether by life or by death, and we must see the overall picture, not just one segment. So we make our will subject to God's will. "If ye abide in me, and my words abide in you, ye shall ask what ye will, and it shall be done unto you" (John 15:7). "And this is the confidence that we have in him, that if we ask any thing according to his will, he heareth us" (I John 5:14). We may have difficulty reconciling these two verses but they are there and, as with divine sovereignty on one hand and human free will on the other, we accept both and leave it to God to harmonize them.

If my dear one recovers, the road may be long and hard. Already over four months of suspense and uncertainty lie behind us. At the beginning of this year, I was much concerned about a closer walk with God and deepening of my spiritual life. Little did I dream of the way God would bring it about! You had better not pray to be conformed to the image of God's Son unless you mean business! It may be anything but the delightful experience you had in mind. God uses strange ways to make us more like Jesus. But they work together for good and the finished product is worth all the cost.

20
The Last Page

When I was a boy I liked to read some of the better novels of the day. I always read the last page first because I wanted to know how it all came out. Then I began at the first page and, although the hero was often in deep trouble and sometimes it looked as though he would not make it through another page, I would say under my breath, "Cheer up, I know the end from the beginning, I've read the last page!"

My Bible is like that. Sometimes in the middle of the book it looks like the devil has it made. "Truth forever on the scaffold, Wrong forever on the throne" (James Russell Lowell). But I've read the last page and there is no devil on it. There is no devil on the first page and no devil on the last page and, although he may strut across the pages between, I know what is coming! Thank God for a Book that disposes of the devil!

So it is with our days on this earth. For the trusting soul God has promised ultimate victory. We see not yet all things put under Him, but we see Jesus. Sin and death, disease, sorrow, and tears are abundant now but one day all these "former things" will have passed away.

I read in my Bible about a pearly white city. Inside it are the saints and without are dogs and sorcerers and whoremongers and murderers and idolaters. Everybody is where he belongs. Satan is in the lake of fire with the beast and false prophet and death and hell. Everything is where it belongs. Things are sadly out of place these days but not forever. I read that Judas went to his own place. Everybody ends up eventually where he belongs.

So now in a vale of shadows I take heart. God will set all things right in His good time. I write this in a motel room in Georgia. How I miss my dear one whose gentle presence made this itinerant ministry so enjoyable! She is awaiting surgery and the outlook is dim. But if I look far enough ahead everything clears up. I've read the last page! There may be some distressing chapters between here and there but somewhere sickness and sorrow and grief and tears will disappear along with the devil. I'm living for that last page!

My *Daily Light* for today reads, "When thou passest through the waters, I will be with thee; and through the rivers, they shall not overflow thee . . . (Isaiah 43:2). On that last page there is a shoreline and fearful as I may sometimes be, I hope to cross the river as old Mr. Fearing did in Pilgrim's Progress, "with the water at a record low and not much above wetshod."

What a dreary journey would this be if we did not have that last page in the Book! There is so much now that defies explanation. But one day everything will be fixed and final. "He that is unjust, let him be unjust still: and he which is filthy, let him be filthy still: and he that is righteous, let him be righteous still: and he that is holy, let him be holy still" (Revelation 22:11). Things do not add up now but one day the facts will all be in, the accounts settled without appeal. Everything and everybody will be where they belong. Don't live for today. Live for that last page!

21

Garrison of Angels

The king of Syria sent troops and horses and chariots to
capture Elisha in Dothan. The prophet's servant looked out
upon soldiers to the right of him, soldiers to the left of him,
here a soldier, there a soldier, everywhere a soldier. In desperation he cried, "How shall we do?" But Elisha looked not down
but up and saw angels to the right of him, angels to the left
of him, here an angel, there an angel, everywhere an angel,
because the angels of the Lord encamped round about him to
deliver him. The prophet of God knew where his defense lay.
He had not underestimated his adversaries but he said,
". . . they that be with us are more than they that be with
them" *(see* 2 Kings 6).

We are sore beset these days but blessed is the man who
correctly estimates his adversaries and his allies. I have heard
of a dog that was always getting into fights and always getting
the worst of it. A friend remarked to the dog's owner, "He's
not much of a fighter." "Oh, no," was the reply, "he's a good
fighter, just a poor judge of dogs!" The Christian, while he does
not underestimate his foes (and nowadays with so much being
said about the devil and demons we are in danger of magnify-
ing the opposition) he correctly numbers his friends and knows
that the odds are on his side.

Paul tells us, "Be careful for nothing; but in everything by
prayer and supplication with thanksgiving let your requests be

made known unto God. And the peace of God, which passeth
all understanding, shall keep [garrison] your hearts and minds
through Christ Jesus" (Philippians 4:6,7). There is our cordon
of angels between us and the demons! This is divine logistics
and we are well guarded. God has provided a garrison for His
people to protect heart and mind. The admonition begins, "Be
careful for nothing." We need not fear or doubt or worry but
rather dismiss all such as of the devil, then pray with thanksgiving for blessings already received or to be received. That paves
the way for a sense of security that believes God is on our side,
however one may feel or however things may appear. Elisha
had that peace but his servant did not and needed to have his
eyes opened. How the troubled saints need such an eye-opener
today! Actually, our primary problem is not light but sight.
Light is of no value to a blind man. Reading books galore on
the subject will not reveal the angels unless our eyes are
touched by faith.

We had better not get so busy counting demons that we
forget the angels. We wrestle not with flesh and blood but as
Ephesians 6:12 PHILLIPS puts it: "We are up against the unseen
power that controls this dark world, and spiritual agents from
the very headquarters of evil." But we are also encompassed by
a heavenly host and we need not fight in this battle for the
battle is the Lord's. We may face the foe with all the confidence of the old captain who, when told that his outfit was
completely surrounded, shouted, "Good, don't let one of them
escape!"

If the Valley is full of your foes, raise your sights to the hills
and see the angels!

22
The Forgotten Beatitude

John the Baptist, the rugged ascetic Elijah of the New Testament, was imprisoned in a dark, dismal, desolate dungeon. It was no place for such an outdoor preacher and his feelings hit a record low. He sent a delegation to Jesus to ask, "Art thou he that should come, or do we look for another?" (Matthew 11:3). That was a record low for John the Baptist. What he had preached like a living exclamation point had become a question mark to the Preacher Himself.

But our Lord did not reprimand the troubled prophet. Instead He made His best statement about John the Baptist on the same day the prophet had made his worst statement about the Lord. And He reminded John that the blind were seeing, the deaf were hearing, the lame were walking, the lepers were being cleansed and the poor were hearing the Gospel. Then He added what is perhaps the most unfamiliar of all the beatitudes, "Blessed is he, whosoever shall not be offended in me" (Matthew 11:6). In other words, "Blessed is he who does not get upset by the way I run my business!"

My Lord is running on schedule. He is carrying out His program according to plans and specifications. He may not be carrying on as we expected. John the Baptist was preaching a Messiah coming in judgment but here was a meek and lowly Jesus going about doing good. God does not operate by our timetable and sometimes it does not add up on our computers.

It is a day of dungeons and many Christians are in the clutches of a giant despair. It may be ill health. It may be bereavement and one's heart lies in a grave. It may be financial. Other things than stone walls can a prison make and other things than iron bars can form a cage. Then there is the distressing world situation. Why doesn't God do something? If He is the Prince of Peace, King of kings, and Lord of lords, why doesn't He come back and clean up this mess? The world is in a dungeon and they are not looking for Jesus, they are looking for another and, as our Lord predicted, there are false Christs and messiahs everywhere.

John the Baptist had announced both the Lamb of God and the coming Messiah. Today my Lord is still carrying on His redemptive work but one day He will return as a lion and set up His Kingdom, establish law and order, and reign in righteousness. I am not looking for another. My Christ has already come and He is coming back. In the meantime He is still doing what He came to do the first time. I have made up my mind to claim the forgotten beatitude. I do not understand all He does and why He does it. The past months have found me often in a dungeon. But I will not be upset or find in Him a stumbling block. He is either a sanctuary or a snare *(See* Isaiah 8:14). I find in Him a Sanctuary. I claim the blessing of the unoffended. Make up your mind that, no matter how the Lord handles your personal problem and no matter how slowly He may seem to end the misery of this evil age, there is a beatitude for saints in dungeons.

23
Longing for a Train Trip

During the past week my dear Sara has shown improvement and I am so happy that I can hardly contain myself. She has a long way to go but her general condition is better, her eyes are brighter, and she shows more interest in everything. She still cannot talk because she has had a tracheotomy and the tube through her nose is bothersome. She writes, however, and her writing has become legible so that we can communicate. She has begun to express very definite feelings about things and that delights me. They say that as long as a woman asks for a mirror there is hope! Sara has not asked for the mirror yet but no doubt she will!

On my way to and from my home to the hospital I pass the old railroad station in Winston-Salem. Passenger service is a thing of the past here but the old station brings pleasant memories. Sara and I came here frequently years ago to take the train to points in the Midwest. I wish we could do it again. My conversion to air travel was not anything to celebrate. There was something about boarding a train on a winter night, going to bed in a comfortable compartment and gliding through the darkness while snow or sleet pelted the windows. Air travel cannot match that! We could see the country instead of maybe just looking down on an ocean of clouds. There was room to walk around and we looked forward to the meals. Oh,

I know there were delays and irritations but the trip was worth it. Train travel represented something unhurried before this poor generation of nervous wrecks could no longer wait. Now maybe it makes little difference whether we see the country or not for do we really see what we see these days?

There are still a few trains and in this frantic congested traffic I cannot dream of a decent reason why train travel should not be reactivated. I know the railroads do not want the passenger business and too many passengers do not want to travel that slowly but in sheer desperation the government might do something. As opposed as I am to governmental controls I would vote for this exception.

If Sara is ever able to travel again I would like to arrange one more train trip on one of the few trains remaining and cross the country as it is still possible to do. I think it would be a red-letter day and at least I dream about it. Maybe I have set my sights pretty high but we can dream. You'll hear about it if we do for that would really be something to write home about!

It is a precious nostalgia that strikes me every time I pass a deserted railroad station. Maybe it is but the sighing of an old man for days beyond recall. But it is also a regret for the passing of a day when life was not so fevered and there was time to view the passing scene. It is only one symptom of a malady that may be terminal and certainly is malignant. We do not usually reverse our course and slow our speed when once we hit the toboggan slide. But I'd like a try at it and I know of no better way to begin the cure than with an old-fashioned train trip like we used to enjoy.

24
The King Knows!

I sit once more in a hospital room beside my dear one while, for her, "Swift to its close ebbs out life's little day." The monitor on the wall registers a feeble heartbeat, next to none. All our hopes and prayers for her recovery have not been answered. We had hoped to see a miracle of healing and to be able to say to a doubting world, "I told you so! God still breaks through!" But I have another message now that may be better: "God makes no mistakes and all He does is right. He has no stereotyped way of doing what He does. He delivered Peter from prison but left John the Baptist in a dungeon to die. I accept whatever He does, however He does it."

One could give way now in a flood of memories, a heart bursting with love while I clasp the hand I have held so often. With the other I would take hold of a sure unfailing Hand, no less real because to sight unseen. This is the time for a sturdy old-time faith that will not shrink though pressed by many a foe. I face the future for life must be lived, whatever is left of it. God would not have us sit up with a corpse. God said to Joshua, "Moses, my servant is dead." What next? "Have a season of mourning?" No! "Now therefore arise, go over this Jordan!" (Joshua 1:2). My Lord said, "Let the dead bury their dead" (Matthew 8:22). Whatever depths of meaning lie hidden there, He means that there is more to do and let us get on with it. There is nothing incogruous in a set jaw along with tear-dimmed eyes. My Lord could weep but He could also set His face toward Jerusalem. There must be time even to laugh in the face of what looks like disaster for life is a strange mixture and if we lose our sense of proportion we shall be like the dear soul who while praying for groceries asked for a barrel of pepper and then exclaimed, "No, Lord, that's too much pepper!" We do not have to choose between cry-baby sentimentalism on one hand and stoicism on the other. Let us just be Christians. Our Lord was perfectly balanced and when He lives within us we shall have some degree of His perfection.

Whoever thinks he has the ways of God conveniently tabulated, analyzed, and correlated with convenient, glib answers to ease every question from aching hearts has not been far in this maze of mystery we call life and death. At this writing I never knew less how to explain the ways of Providence but I never had more confidence in my God.

During the London blitz of World War II many children were evacuated to the country by order of the government. As one load pulled out, someone asked a youngster, "Where are you going?" He replied, "I don't know BUT THE KING KNOWS!" I don't know where I'm headed or what lies out there. BUT MY KING KNOWS and I have one ambition left, to be His faithful subject

25
Until

My joy at Sara's turn for the better was short-lived. Even the doctors and nurses thought she was "over the hill" but a stroke was too much after all the blows of weeks past. She left us on Sunday morning. A few days before, she had been scribbling a few things on a pad since she could not speak. One of them was, "My future looks dark." It does not look dark now. She has entered an eternal sunrise where night never falls.

I have not lost her for I know where she is!

> Death can hide but not divide;
> Thou art but on Christ's other side;
> Thou are with Christ and Christ with me,
> United still in Christ are we.
>
> AUTHOR UNKNOWN

She also wrote: "I have had to endure many things (she did not mean her treatment in the hospital for that was magnificent)—I have had to endure many things that I cannot tell you until . . ." and there she stopped. But when we meet again she will not tell me for one minute of heaven has already erased all the sorrow and suffering she ever endured. I am waiting, however, for the great "Until"—". . . until the Lord come" (1 Corinthians 4:5); ". . . until the times of the Gentiles be

fulfilled" (Luke 21:24); "Until he that hindereth be taken out
of the way" *(see* 2 Thessalonians 2:7); ". . . till he hath put all
enemies under his feet" (1 Corinthians 15:25); "Until he sub-
dues all things unto himself" *(see* Philippians 3:21). A friend
of mine, after hearing me preach along this line on Living In
The Great Until, ended his letter to me not "Yours truly" but
just "Until!"

I have not long to go until—I'm living for that. And she who
was dearest on earth will make heaven dearer. For five months
we did not get to talk much and we will have all eternity to
catch up.

We laid Sara to rest in a quaint Quaker cemetery, serene and
peaceful, in keeping with her Quaker tradition. Away from
noise and tumult it breathes the spirit of John Greenleaf Whittier's immortal lines from "The Eternal Goodness."

> I know not what the future hath
> Of marvel or surprise,
> Assured alone that life and death,
> His mercy underlies;
> And if my heart and flesh are weak
> To bear an untried pain,
> The bruised reed He will not break,
> But strengthen and sustain.

Sara did no public speaking but once I persuaded her to
record and recite on tape another of the Quaker poet's master-
pieces, "To Paths Unknown," that ends with a longing for
heaven:

There, from the music round about me stealing,
I fain would learn the new and holy song,
And find at last, beneath Thy trees of healing,
The life for which I long.

She lives now beneath those trees of healing. I plod along,
a lonely pilgrim, numb with the loss of her companionship but
confident of the truth of one more Whittier verse from "The
Eternal Goodness."

I know not where His islands lift
Their fronded palms in air;
I only know I cannot drift
Beyond His love and care.

JOHN GREENLEAF WHITTIER

26
Gone

No matter how one may condition himself for the passing of a dear one, no matter how many weeks or months to get ready for the actual moment, there comes the inevitable shock and the grim final blow when you realize that the one most precious is no longer here. I find myself saying under my breath again and again though ever so softly, "Sara is gone."

Gone with her are a thousand other precious things that made the past years so delightful. Gone the anticipation of returning home to be greeted at the airport or the apartment door. Gone the thrill of hearing that voice at the other end of the telephone call and the cheery "Hey, Honey!" Gone those airmail letters in the motel box, one every day. Gone the clasp of that dear hand as we strolled about all over the country. Gone that lovely face in the congregation, smiling at my jokes she had heard countless times. Gone—and the chilling, numbing awareness that it can never be again down here. So I stumble along in my grief, mumbling under my breath, "Sara's gone."

But God is not gone, the Book is not gone, the blessed Holy Spirit called alongside to help is not gone, and Jesus is here. After all, we know where Sara is, just a little farther along, just over the border. And what business has an old septuagenarian, now threescore and twelve, moaning when he himself can't possibly be around much longer? Anybody that near to the next world, that close to heaven, need not lament as though a lifetime lay between him and his destination! This little boot camp is about over, this internship is almost past, and "His servants shall serve him there" *(see* Revelation 22:3). Sara has just been promoted to a higher grade and I stand in line—and not far down that line. She has just gone and I am going!

One of these days the picture will change. What is gone will be present and what is so present now will have disappeared. We will join our loved ones again and forever. William Jennings Bryan said, "Christ has made of death a narrow, starlit strip between the companionships of yesterday and the reunions of tomorrow." Where will tears be then? Gone, for God will have wiped them away. What happened to death? Gone! What about sorrow? Gone! And crying? Gone! And what happened to pain, that old companion of these days? Gone! ". . . for the former things are passed away" (Revelation 21:4). And what happened to the devil? Gone. And sin that has blighted our world these centuries? Gone. Where are the wicked? Gone to where they belong. What became of darkness and night? Gone. Instead, eternal day and all the saints and angels and the river of life and the tree of life and the throne of God and Jesus on it. All that has gone will be present and all that is so painfully present will be gone.

So, dear one, you are not gone, just gone on ahead. And I would say, in lines precious to me:

> Should you go first and I remain,
> One thing I'd have you do:
> Walk slowly down the path of death,
> For soon I'll follow you.

I'll want to know each step you take
I'll want to walk the same,
For some day down that lonely road
You'll hear me call your name.

ALBERT ROWSWELL

27
Off on a Third Venture

This morning, all alone in my apartment, I am packing up to start out on the third phase of my ministry. For nearly twenty-five years I was a bachelor preacher. Then followed thirty-three precious years with Sara by my side. Now, almost seventy-two, I take to the road as a wandering widower. My confidence is that God will make up to me all that my dear one meant and infinitely more for I am shut up to Him, and the soul that on Jesus has leaned for repose He will not desert to its foes.

There is only one possible way to make it home through the dangers, toils, and snares of these last days of my little span and, I believe, the last days of the age before my Lord returns. That is the way of the simple faith, the pilgrim character, and the blessed hope. Childlike trust in Jesus, the conscious appropriation of the living Christ for every need, tasting in advance the powers of the age to come, not standing on Jordan's stormy banks casting a wishful eye toward Canaan but dwelling now in Beulah Land, the believer's rest in God's finished work in Christ. Only a vital, vivid, victorious faith can see us through. I do not mean a tense pose we screw ourselves up to and strain to maintain but a calm trust that the Lord is my Shepherd and my times are in His hand.

And I must ever remember that I am an exile and an alien in this world, a stranger and a pilgrim just passing through. The fashion of this world is passing away and I am in it but not of it. Dr. Phillips says in his preface to *Letters to Young Churches* to the early Christians that this world was only a part. Therefore, they trained themselves not to be "taken in" by this world, nor to give their hearts to it, and not to conform to its values, but to remember always that they were only temporary residents with their rights of citizenship in the unseen world.

Finally, I want to make my way in joyous expectation that Jesus may come back any day and if He delays, then:

> One sweetly solemn thought
> Comes to me o'er and o'er;
> I'm nearer home today
> Than I've ever been before.
> PHOEBE CARY

It can't be long, either way for as the old hymn puts it, "The strife will soon be o'er."

Cheap faith, mouthing pet clichés, occasional spurts in devo-

tions, these will never do it now. The powers of evil are step-
ping up the pressure, the sands of time run low.

> My soul, be on thy guard;
> Ten thousand foes arise;
> The hosts of sin are pressing hard
> To draw thee from the skies.
>
> GEORGE HEATH

Once when I quoted this I put it "A thousand foes arise."
George Heath did not overestimate the adversaries! But they
that be with us are more than they that be with them. Gird
yourself, brother, with simple faith, pilgrim character, and the
blessed hope and let us be going!

28
Lonely

I sit alone in Washington National Airport. All these years I have traveled but never has loneliness descended upon me as now. I find myself instinctively, subconsciously looking around as though my dear Sara ought to be somewhere near as she used to be, reading a magazine, just waiting, happy to be with me. I traveled for years before I met Sara but this is not like that. Now I've had her and she is gone. And the frightening knowledge that I can't call her when I get to Detroit or find her waiting when I return home chills the marrow of my bones. If ever I needed her it is now and it is hard to repress the insistent "Why?" No poor man like this ever needed a woman like that more than I do in these declining years. But no answer is available so I lay it all on the shelf for future reference.

This world was never more unattractive than today. These hurrying throngs of strangers with not a familiar face in the crowd—what a heartless world it can be for who knows or cares! I never wanted to leave it like I do this afternoon but my time is not yet so I breathe a feeble prayer and recruit my limited resources. ". . . my strength is made perfect in weakness," God has said (2 Corinthians 12:9) and I can say, ". . . when I am weak, then am I strong" (12:10). By that rule I should be a colossus now for I've never been weaker. I do not question my Father who is making all things work together for good to those who love Him and are the called according to His purpose. And what is that purpose? To be conformed to the image of God's Son, to be made like Jesus. It takes a lot of time and doing to make such stubborn, faulty lumps of clay into a vessel that He can use.

The new hilarious brand of Christianity is only a better way to have a good time. Fun seems to be the objective but wrestling with powers and principalities doesn't sound much like fun. Wrestling isn't fun to start with and when the foe is the devil it is not exactly recreation. The new breed of Christians knows little of the power of His Resurrection, the fellowship of His sufferings, and conformity to His death, the very things Paul wanted to know.

If these desolate days are part of the process of making me more usable to God for whatever time is left and a greater blessing to others, I accept them and gladly submit my poor clay to the hand of the Potter. God forbid that I ever sing again as glibly as most of us have,

> Mold me and make me
> After Thy will
> While I am waiting,
> Yielded and still.
>
> ADELAIDE A. POLLARD

How few have ever been yielded and fewer still have been still! Forgive me for asking, "Why?" Forgive the petulance, the rebel sigh. "Hold o'er my being absolute sway."

29
Account Closed

Today I have been trying to get my little finances together now that I'm starting life alone again without Sara. I've been tranferring her bank and savings accounts over to mine. It is not happy business but one of those things that has to be done. The kind lady at the bank and another at the savings office gave me the books my dear will not need any more and over the front she wrote "Closed." I laid them away with a pain in my heart as I thought how through the years we had always divided our income and thanked the Lord for the way it always came in. Now it is all mine but the debit side outweighs the credit, for much of the joy departs when there is no one with whom you can share it. It's like coming home as I do now with no one to come home to.

But I've been doing a little thinking about my dear one's closed accounts. She had another account laid up where moth and rust cannot corrupt nor thieves break through and steal. It must be a tidy sum by now for she started making heavenly deposits early and the interest runs high. There never was any worry about inflation or bankruptcy for depressions never reach that fair land. She must be cashing in on it heavily by now and the reserves will never be exhausted. While I bother with taxes and forms and inventories down here in this world of red tape where I am only a number, cataloged from *A* to *Z*, auto license to zip code, Sara revels in the wealth of glory and eats at the banquets of God. Dear darling, you had another account that can't be closed and they don't keep any books up there. You have joined the aristocracy of heaven and, compared to it, the posh millionaires' clubs of earth are but beggars counting their pennies. I'll join you shortly and it will be a welcome relief from filling out blanks down here trying to render unto Caesar the things that are Caesar's.

My sweetheart was rich down here in things that money can't buy and up there they have no other wealth. Her little books look sad as I lay them away and there is a tug at my lonely heart but I'm happy, too, for the hand of death and disaster can never close accounts where she has gone.

I miss her dreadfully but I cannot really wish her back but rather mend my step and hasten on to overtake her. For years we attended a supper here where I gave the Christmas message. When she lay ill I walked often by the meeting place and prayed that we might sit together once more at that supper. It was not to be—but there is another supper coming up at the Marriage of the Lamb. We've been invited and we'll be there. We'll be citizens in a new realm where time is not reckoned in years nor wealth in money. It will be an everlasting celebration and we'll sit at the King's table with angels to furnish the music.

Better start a heavenly lay-away plan and invest in eternity. They never close the accounts over there.

30
Something Better

I had hoped for the miraculous healing of Sara and that we might bear a dramatic testimony to the direct intervention of God. I had a sermon ready. But it was not to be. My dearest died in spite of the day-and-night efforts of a medical center equipped with the very latest and best in machines, medicine, and methods. It did not please God to heal her. Instead she succumbed to a terrible malady that distorted and disfigured her fair face and features so that we did not open the casket at the funeral.

My disappointment was intense but sober thinking has changed my view. If a dramatic experience of healing had been ours it would have been sensational, but such experiences are rare and my listeners and readers would have said, "That is very wonderful but it happens only once in a while and is the exception that proves the rule. Most of us do not have such miracles. Our loved ones die, our hopes fade, and we need a word for those who walk the Valley with no happy ending to the story." I can see now that God denied me what I sought that I might bring a message to the multitude like myself whose prayers were not answered as hoped.

The Book of Job ends with Job richer than ever in earthly blessings, but not all of God's saints come to such a prosperous finish. Some of the best Christians do not spend their last days in a rocking chair serenely enjoying a blissful sunset. Many a dear old mother ends her course with children still unsaved. Some go out under a mental cloud. Others are no longer able to carry on their work and languish like John the Baptist in prison until they almost wonder as did he concerning the Lord, "Art Thou He that should come or look we for another?" So I preach and write for a host of fellow travelers through the Valley whose hopes, like mine, were not realized and whose deepest wish was not granted. If we can move through this Valley and come out in victory, we have found a greater blessing than if our personal wish had been fulfilled in some miraculous way.

After all, we were not saved to be made happy but to be made holy. That requires a refining process that may be costly but is worth any price. Our Saviour walked through a Valley that ended with a cross but He came out of it on a Resurrection morning—and so shall we! We shall regain our loved ones under better conditions than if God had spared them for a few more days in this vale of tears. We have really lost nothing because what we longed for has not been denied, only deferred, to be enjoyed forever.

During the past weeks a host of dear people have gripped my hand and often with tears in their eyes have let me know that they, too, have walked through this Valley. Their wishes too were not granted in the way they hoped. If I had been able to tell a different story—and I thank God for those who can—it would have put me in a different category and we would not be playing on the same string. I am now companion to a multitude who know bereavement and sorrow and who wait

with me for fulfillment still ahead. Heaven means more and we
fear death less and the river beckons us instead of repelling us
because our heart is on the other side.

31
It Has Come to That

In one of my books I have written about the old lady who
was told that the doctors had done all they could and now she
must trust the Lord. "My soul," she moaned, "has it come to
that!"

In my loneliness, facing old age with the frightening prospect of no one to care for me, I have been tempted to join the
old lady in her fears. I have come to that, just trusting the Lord.
Does it not always come to that? Since it does, shouldn't we
start with that instead of coming to it as a last resort? Whom
have we in heaven or on earth but God? I am not the first to
travel without a helpmeet. They have been doing it since Paul
set the example. I thank God for many close friends these days
but in the last analysis I am shut up to the Lord. I have no
explanation of why I am left alone when I need most my dear
one for these declining years. Humanly, we may grow a bit

uneasy at times but there comes the blessed assurance that
Jesus lives within, the Holy Spirit is our companion, and our
Father watches over us. That is safety and security and I say
with the Scotsman, "Who ever heard of anybody drowning
with his head that high above water!"

I have read of a mountain traveler who was walking near a
dangerous precipice at night. His foot slipped and he grabbed
a bush to hang on for dear life, fearing that he was hanging over
the abyss. His grip finally gave out and he fell—just a few
inches to solid ground below! Some of us cliff-hangers fancy we
are over the precipice and hang on in frantic desperation.
When we finally "let go and let God" we find underneath the
Everlasting Arms.

Eventually every man must face his God, and since it comes
to that we might as well start with it. If we remember our
Creator in the days of our youth we shall be ready for everything as it comes and not face a long-deferred confrontation
in some grave crisis or at death's door. Enoch walked with God
and his translation was just the last phase of a glorious pilgrimage. Somebody has said that Enoch walked so close to God that
time just merged into eternity. God said, "Come, share the day
with me" and since there is no night there, Enoch has been
spending the day ever since!

When all the props are knocked out we feel a heavenly
helplessness. At first we may tremble but then we begin to take
stock and find we are on the firmest footing we have ever
known. God hung the earth on nothing and He can keep us
in what looks like thin air. Insomniacs cannot sleep until they
stop holding up the bed and let the bed support them.

Don't wait until some emergency brings you to cast yourself upon God just because you can't do anything else anyway. It always comes to that—so start with it. It was never meant to be a last resort. Like the Bible, our lives ought to start with "In the beginning God. . . ." Jesus is Alpha and Omega, the First and the Last, the Beginning and the End. That makes full circle, "And ye are complete in him . . ." (Colossians 2:10).

32
More Unanswered Questions

When my dear one fell ill, a verse in my *Daily Light* read, "This sickness is not unto death, but for the glory of God that the Son of God might be glorified thereby" (John 11:4). I know that we cannot put our finger down on a verse every time and accept what we find as guidance for a course of action. One preacher made much of a verse in book of daily devotions that said, "Arise ye and depart for this is not your rest" (Micah 2:10). He took it as orders to leave his church and seek a new pastorate. Then he reflected that if he followed that leading he would have to move every year when that verse came around again!

But I do not accept the opposite view that these verses in our daily readings are only accidents of the printer with no special significance. Many a time a certain passage has been one way God guides us on a definite day with a definite problem. At any rate I claimed my verse for Sara's illness and clung to it for five months. But her sickness WAS unto death.

She herself believed that she would be healed, that she would not have a relapse of her ailment. She had all the faith she could muster and was as sure as she could be. Several Christian friends were of like conviction. We anointed her, we had a special season of prayer when we claimed the promise that if two agreed as touching what they would ask, God would do it. With mustard-seed faith we bade the mountain move and endeavored not to doubt. But the mountain did not move, my dear one had a relapse and left us. We had done everything we knew to do, not perfectly, but as best we could.

I have no easy explanation. I know that what we will must be within the wider circle of what God wills. Some ask, "How can we pray AND NOT DOUBT if we are not certain that what we ask is God's will? And indeed why pray at all if God is going to do what He wills anyway?" Well, we are told that we have not because we ask not and there are many blessings that might be ours if we asked for them and sometimes that includes healing. Because a father knows what is best for his child and does not see fit to grant every request does not preclude the child from making its wishes known. There are things my father never would have given me if I hadn't asked for them. It is both our duty and our privilege to make our requests known to God subject to His will.

I do not have all the answers to why Sara's childlike and unshaken faith for healing was not rewarded. It certainly is an answer to cheap and glib extremism on the subject. On the other hand, it does not mean that miracles of healing do not occur, for they do. What it does mean is that we accept what does happen and table all dogmatic assertions on the subject until we have better light. And when we do, we shall not even bother to ask why, for all will be forgotten in the glory of His presence.

33
Now Thee Alone

God is the Rewarder of them that diligently seek Him *(see* Hebrews 11:6). But He said to Abraham, "I am thy shield and thy exceeding great reward" (Genesis 15:1). Most of us think of God only as our Rewarder. We make a Santa Claus of the Almighty, seeking His gifts but not Himself. Someone has said that the difference between Patrick Henry and the average American is that he said, "Give me liberty or give me death" and today we say, "Gimme. . . ."

Our Lord emphasized the fact that following Him must take

precedence over loved ones, lands, and life itself. Tone it down as you will, He would have us really mean it when we sing, "Jesus Is All the World to Me." Paul says that we must be as though we had no wives, as though we rejoiced or wept not, as though we bought not nor used this world. Sometimes dear ones are taken, health fails us, possessions are lost, and all to drive us to God Himself. Christ must fill the picture and all else must be "in the Lord," a phrase used much in the New Testament. The average Christian shuts the Lord up in one room of his heart and brings Him out only on Sunday or in a crisis. He worships at another shrine. But our God is a jealous God and will not share His throne with another.

However, we do not really lose everything, for when we belong to Christ all things are ours—life, death, the world, things present and to come. Like Paul we have nothing and possess all things. But we no longer have the "gimmes." We can sing:

> Once earthly joy I craved,
> Sought peace and rest;
> Now Thee alone I seek,
> Give what is best.
>   ELIZABETH PRENTISS

Then, anything He sends will be all right. We have Him and ". . . by him all things consist" (Colossians 1:17); "And ye are complete in him . . ." (2:10). That is fulfillment and it cannot be found anywhere else.

Our lives should follow the pattern of the Lord's Prayer. We begin with His name, His Kingdom, and His will. Then we get around to "Give us this day our daily bread" and all our other needs. When He Himself is our Reward we leave the lesser rewards to Him.

I have read of a business executive who was besieged in his office all day by people seeking favors. Near the close of that long day his little son came to the office. "And what is it that you want?" the father asked good-naturedly.

The youngster replied, "I don't want anything, I just came to be with you."

I believe our Heavenly Father would appreciate it if, for a change, we came to Him in prayer, not asking for favors, but seeking only His fellowship.

When we seek Him alone we end up with all else we need, for if we seek first the Kingdom of God and His righteousness, then all these things shall be added unto us.

34
I Trust His Heart

Today at lunch a friend of mine told me that Spurgeon said that God is too good to be unkind, too wise to be mistaken, and when you cannot trace His hand, you can always trust His heart. I have been through much that I do not understand. God does not ask me to understand it but to accept it. He is saying, "What I do thou knowest not now; but thou shalt know hereafter" (John 13:7).

I cannot trace His hand but I can trust His heart. I know that God is love and back of all His doings is that love. It sent His Son into this world and reached its climax on Calvary. It is the hallmark of His disciples. "We know that we have passed from death unto life, because we love the brethren" (1 John 3:14). "By this shall all men know that ye are my disciples, if ye have love one to another" (John 13:35). WE know and ALL MEN know that we are His because His love is shed abroad in our hearts by the Holy Spirit. It is inward evidence and outward evidence. I know that whom the Lord loveth He chasteneth. His corrective discipline proves my sonship.

Back of all the misery and mystery of this world beats that heart of love. I cannot trace God's hand in news reports and the happenings in this modern madhouse. Satan is on the loose.

Careless seems the great Avenger;
   history's pages but record
One death-grapple in the darkness
   'twixt old systems and the Word;
Truth forever on the scaffold,
   Wrong forever on the throne,—
Yet that scaffold sways the future,
   and, behind the dim unknown,
Standeth God within the shadow,
   keeping watch above his own.
                JAMES RUSSELL LOWELL

Let me keep step with the heartbeat of God and that heart-beat is love. I believe that I have reached to some degree that rest I sought at the first of this year. There remains much land to be possessed and I do not count myself to have attained but I am on my way. I did not dream what lay ahead. I do not fathom nor can I explain my Father's dealings. But I find no rebellion in my soul and know that all of it is working together for good.

I cannot always trace His hand but I can trust His heart. And His heart directs His hand. If I trust the heart I need never question the hand. They never contradict each other.

35
The Supreme Bereavement

One thing is certain when your dearest leaves you for heaven and you plod on alone—there can be no harder blow, no greater human bereavement. After this any other adversities, any other tragedies, any other disasters will be secondary. You have had the worst. Whatever happens to you personally is incidental. Much of the darkness of death disappears for it becomes the door to a glad reunion.

I speak of husbands and wives who really loved each other and were as one. Marriage today has become a cheap and temporary arrangement and millions separate without waiting for death to part them. There is no heartache, no bitter loneliness, no tear in the eye or choke in the throat, no tender memories that wrench the feelings and numb the soul. They wouldn't know what I mean.

But there is this balm for the wound, this compensation, we have had the worst. Anything else that can happen will be a lesser evil. This is the ultimate in tribulation.

I speak, mind you, of things we cannot control and on the human level. There is a greater disaster possible in things spiritual. When trouble comes, we can backslide, lose our faith and our testimony, become rebels against the providence of God. Satan would overthrow us either as a roaring lion, an angel of light, or as the Great Accuser. He uses bereavement

and adversity to depress our spirits, divert us from God's best
until we become disapproved castaways. This is worse than any
earthly loss. But if we maintain our faith through tribulation,
no other earthly loss can be as great as parting from our other
half.

How important that we make the most of the years we have
together so that our loneliness will not be made darker by
regrets! In the last letter she wrote to me on the day she
entered the hospital my dear one wrote, "You've always been
so faithful." I'd rather have that line than anything else she
could have written. It reminds me of the last words my old
mother sent to me: "Tell Vance to keep up the good fight, for
God is with him and if God be for us, who can be against us?"
Is not faithfulness, old-fashioned loyalty, the virtue that outlasts all other attributes and will endure when looks and glam-
our and brilliance and success have faded? God thinks a lot of
it for it is the one requirement of His stewards and at the Last
Day the supreme reward will be, "Well done, thou good and
faithful servant" (Matthew 25:21).

If you have been true to your dearest and to your God, any
temporary loss can be borne in hope of a glorious future when
we are joined again with those who reached heaven ahead of
us. Meanwhile, we have had the worst blow that trouble can
deliver and we can use it to comfort others with the comfort
wherewith we are comforted of God.

There is not much that I dread from here on out. When one
has drained the bitterest cup he is better prepared for any other
potion that life may serve. Indeed he can sing:

Let sorrow do its work,
Send grief or pain;
Sweet are Thy messengers,
Sweet their refrain,
When they can sing with me:
More love, O Christ, to Thee,
More love to Thee! More love to Thee!

ELIZABETH P. PRENTISS

36
God of the Living

When the Sadducees asked our Lord about the woman who had had seven husbands and wanted to know whose wife would she be in the resurrection, He answered by analyzing their trouble as error born of ignorance—ignorance of the Scriptures and the power of God. He declared that in the resurrection we neither marry nor are given in marriage but are as the angels in heaven. Then He gave them God's own word, "I am the God of Abraham, Isaac and Jacob" and ended with the declaration, "God is not the God of the dead, but of the living" *(see* Matthew 22:32).

God did not say, "I WAS the God of Abraham, Isaac and Jacob but "I AM. . . ." Always the great I AM whose infinitudes never put Him in the past tense, in His sight nobody WAS but everybody IS. Nobody is dead and everybody who has ever lived is still living.

We are so accustomed to think of the dead as corpses lying in graveyards. But those bodies are only the remains, the temporary vehicles of their earthly stay. They themselves are still in existence somewhere. Moses and Elijah came back to the Mount of Transfiguration and the disciples recognized them. That raises questions as to what we will be like after death and before the resurrection but settles one major issue, we will still be living somewhere. God is not the God of the dead but of the living.

I found a dirt road behind the motel where I am staying this week in Michigan. I've been walking in the glorious September sunshine meditating on the God of the living. He does not deal in dead things. My loved ones are all alive on the other side. One of these days the trumpet will sound and their spirits will be joined to their new resurrection bodies and death will be swallowed up in victory. What a big swallow that will be! Corpses and funerals and cemeteries will be a thing of the past and we shall gather around the throne of the living God, the God of the living. He is the Author of life and there never would have been any death had not the devil invaded creation. But on that day Satan and his cohorts will be where they belong and we shall meet at the river of life around the tree of life to enjoy life everlasting.

But I need not wait for that day for my eternal life to begin. It started when I trusted my Saviour and I have it as surely as

I will ever have it, though not as completely as when I see my Lord on that "Great Getting-up Morning." But now I have the promise of my inheritance and the foretaste of glory divine and if this be the first installment, what will it be like when I am paid in full! Until then I shall taste the powers of the age to come and work up an appetite for the Supper of the Lamb where the celebration never ends.

I worship the God of the living. My soul is not dwelling in the macabre realm of tombs and ghosts. Everybody past and present is alive. All who died in Christ are more alive than ever, they are but on His other side. We need to "come alive" in our thinking and walk with God in His Everlasting Now.

37
Some Things to Remember

The three Hebrew children faced the fiery furnace with unshaken faith: "Our God whom we serve is able to deliver us from the burning fiery furnace." Then they added, "But if not, be it known unto thee, O king, that we will not serve thy gods, nor worship the golden image which thou hast set up" (Daniel 3:17, 18). There was no doubt that God COULD deliver. Whether or not He WOULD was in His hands. So they made provision for the possibility that He might not. But if He should not deliver them FROM the furnace, He would deliver them IN the furnace and, come what might, they would be true to Him.

It is well to be prepared for the IF NOTS. God does not always spare us trouble. Indeed in the world we shall have tribulation (pressure). But when it comes He will be with us in it. There was Another with the Hebrew children in the fiery furnace, the Fourth in the fire. And the form of the Fourth was like the Son of God. There is Another with us in life's fiery furnace and He is the Son of God. He suffered being tempted and is able to succor them that are tempted. He is with us all the days even unto the end of the age. He will not leave us or forsake us. The Comforter, the One called alongside to help is by our side. Whether God will deliver us FROM the furnace or IN it is in His hands. We will be true, whatever happens. We will not bow to the gods of this age or its images.

Never has the pressure to worship other gods been so terrific. Never has the world bowed before so many images as today. It is the thing to do and he who does not grovel before these deities faces a fiery furnace. The temper of the times is against him. The furnace of devilish hostility is being heated seven times hotter than ever before. We shall be snubbed and scorned, called oddballs, squares, throwbacks, obscurantists. God is able to spare us from the furnace but if not He will join us in it. Whether He spare or share He will be there.

On the voyage to Rome, Paul advised his companions at sea that all would be spared, only the ship would be lost. He was in touch with heaven and angels. So he said, ". . . be of good cheer: for I believe God, that it shall be even as it was told me. Howbeit we must be cast upon a certain island" (Acts 27:25, 26). God has assured us today that we shall make it to our heavenly destination but there are some islands between here and there, and we had better be ready for the HOWBEITS.

Furthermore, our assurance of a safe arrival does not allow us to do as we please. When the crewmen were about to flee the ship Paul said, "Except these abide in the ship, ye cannot be saved" (27:31). He had already said that everybody would be saved but if they did not follow instructions they would not be saved. If we are predestinated to make it safe to shore we are not thereby permitted to flee the ship at our own discretion. Within God's sovereignty lies personal responsibility.

Let us remember the IF NOTS and the HOWBEITS. Then we shall not fear the furnace nor flee the ship ahead of time.

38
The Buick

I never owned an automobile until I was sixty-six. Sara took driving lessons and we bought the Buick. We agreed that she would drive and I would pray! She drove better than I prayed, for I usually went to sleep and was a poor copilot. But what a happy time we had for five years, especially on our preaching trips and our visits to the mountains! We loved the Blue Ridge Parkway. I enjoyed leaving the big highways to travel country roads. Sara became an authority on car driving and I used to say that I wished I knew my New Testament like she knew her Buick manual!

A month ago my dear one went to heaven. I do not drive a car and have no intention of learning how to stay alive in the maniac traffic of today. So I sold the Buick and it will leave today. I am not going to watch the new owner drive off with it. I am a sentimental poor soul and with nobody watching I will probably shed some tears as I have already done. Sara and the Buick were parts of one dear picture. She kept it spotless and lavished on it attention and care that few automobiles have ever had. People marvelled at it and it is the best secondhand buy on record by my calculation.

I know I'm supposed to view it simply as a business deal but I don't. So many tender memories are wrapped around that car that it almost has personality of its own. And to lose it so soon after Sara left us is compounded sorrow and added bereavement. Another sweet chapter is forever closed. But I have much to be thankful for. We had our trip to Europe and the Holy Land before disaster descended. She lived long enough to get her picture with me in my book *Threescore and Ten*. God always makes things come out right.

And let me tell you of another precious providence from the Father's hand. I dreaded the thought of the Buick falling into the hands of somebody who would not give it the care it had received. I am preaching this week in a church nearby and, would you believe it, a dear couple, friends of mine from earlier meetings in Florida, came through on a vacation trip, stopped to hear me, heard about the Buick, and bought it! It couldn't be in better hands. So my pain is tempered by the comfort that the old buggy will end its days in the best of circumstances. The Lord knew how much I could stand so He sent the right people along at the right time. He is always doing things like that for His children.

I treasure a little snapshot of my dear one standing beside the Buick up on the Parkway. Only I know what blessed recollections gather round it. But we shall all soon lay aside the vehicles of our earthly pilgrimage for a better land where God uses chariots and angels for transportation. I don't know just how Sara and I will get around up there but you may be sure it will be heavenly and we may even reminisce a bit about the old days down below. Cars end up in junkyards but, thank God, we don't. Meanwhile, I'll get along as best I can without Sara and the Buick but I can't help the lump in my throat this morning.

39
Heart to Heart

The trials and tribulations of the past months are beginning to pay off. In my recent meetings there has been a new note in my messages and a new response from my hearers. It is not mere sympathy with me in my sorrow. There have never been so many troubled and burdened hearts as today and they feel a kinship with one who has been walking through the Valley. Young and old have pressed forward to grasp my hand. Heart answers heart, we stand on common ground and speak the same language.

A church congregation can look like an assemblage of comfortable people without a trouble in the world. The Sunday morning mask is particularly deceptive. But if one speaks from experience and not from observation, if he "sits where they sit," he will learn that there are not many in any such gathering who have not been bruised and battered in life's conflicts and many with broken hearts not revealed by the face.

The Saviour had compassion on the multitude. Sympathy is about the same word with Greek origin instead of Latin. But neither means just feeling sorry for somebody. They mean entering into their troubles, being able to share with them because you have been there. You are not handing out worn clichés from reading and observation. People sense it when you speak from the heart. The simplest testimony may say what a profound sermon might never get across. Our Lord was tempted in all points as we are. He walked our road.

In my early ministry I was inclined sometimes to be rather sarcastic. The Bible tells us that Ephraim was "a cake not turned" *(see* Hosea 7:8). Pity an Ephraim in the ministry who tries to be hard-boiled to hide the fact that he is only half-baked! A few years in the oven of God's chastening will work wonders.

I have paid a great price for a new note in my preaching. When God consumes the dross and refines the gold in His children, they feel it. When He operates He does not use an anesthetic. He does not develop His saints in their sleep. We wrestle with the powers of darkness and we do not come from a wrestling match looking like we had just left a dress parade, well tailored and perfumed. Artificial flowers may look better than real flowers because they have not been exposed to wind and rain. God is not out primarily to make us happy but to make us holy—and holiness is not cheap.

There is compensation for our suffering if we are enabled to comfort others with our own comfort.

> An overflowing heart if thou
> Another's soul would reach;
> An overflowing heart it is
> That gives the lips full speech.
> AUTHOR UNKNOWN

One does not learn to sing or speak from the heart in the schools of men. He finds it in the school of suffering but it pays off in the joy of sharing the Saviour's ministry to heal the brokenhearted, proclaim liberty to the captives, recovery of sight to the blind, and setting at liberty the bruised.

40
The Third Dimension

Christian experience runs on three levels. There are those rare high days when we climb the utmost heights and catch a gleam of glory bright. the mountaintop days. I have had some such days and I thank God for them but they are few and far between and we cannot live on that level as some try to do, bounding from one peak to another with long intervals in the valleys between. Whoever said that nothing is more dangerous to true Christian experience than too many experiences must have had this in mind. Paul's trip to the third heaven is very interesting but he did not major on such high moments.

Then there are the ordinary days, the usual grind when we neither fly nor walk but run and sometimes that requires more grace than the times of trial and trouble. The maid who complained that her work was so "daily" put it well.

But there is a third dimension and we had better recognize

it and be ready for it. There are those chapters in our book that
do not make sense, when weird and uncanny things happen,
when prayers are not answered and our requests are refused,
and we are hard pressed by strange Satanic forces. The Enemy
comes in like a flood and the powers of darkness make mockery
of our faith. All the books we had read fail us and our last page
does not end "happily ever after." Doubts and fears assail the
soul and one thinks of Jeremiah crying, "Wilt thou be al-
together unto me as a liar, and as waters that fail?" (Jeremiah
16:18).

We might as well face the third dimension. There is no
explanation for much of it and some grow bitter trying to add
it all up on their little computers. We must remember that we
live in a world wrecked by sin where Satan still wreaks his
havoc. Things do not run a smooth, orderly course and everything, like the weather, is subject to crazy aberrations. There
is much that makes neither rhyme nor reason. Back of it all
stands God, within the shadow, keeping watch above His own,
but our Lord has not yet returned to set up law and order. We
must face this disordered world as it is, walking by faith and
not by sight. The highest achievement is to trust God anyway
even when the facts laugh in our face and only the grim law
of cause and effect seems to work and divine intervention
seems a thing of the past.

The best of God's saints have had their days and even years
in the third dimension and have come through to victory. Our
Lord Himself met Gethsemane and Golgotha but He mastered
death and the grave and became the Firstborn of that new race
that shall one day break through to that blessed fourth dimen-

sion in the life to come—to reign with the Saviour in a world redeemed and reclaimed where things really add up and we live happily ever after.

Be ready for that hour when best-laid plans crack up and nothing makes sense. Remember that just because they do not make sense to you does not mean that they do not make sense at all. Remember that you are seeing the ragged side of the tapestry and that from heaven it looks entirely different. That bit of weaving that looked so senseless on the bottom side but when turned over, reads: "GOD IS LOVE" is a fair illustration. And from that side all things are working together for our good if we are His.

41
No Home Down Here

Sara's favorite song was a little-known simple thing: "This World Is Not My Home, I'm Only Passing Through." It certainly fitted her life-style for with her Quaker background and her careful habits she was indeed a stranger and a pilgrim down here. Always neat, trim, and well dressed, she never looked like a woman of this world. She wore her hair long and her hemlines were below the decree of the stylists. Buying clothes became an ordeal in the last years when Sodom and Gomorrah set the pace for indecency and immodesty.

I am now a lonely pilgrim with her no more by my side but I can sing her song from my heart. If you are in love with this world, brother, you can have it! It has lost whatever charm it had for me. By this world I do not mean the earth or its people but the present world order in its final degeneracy. I grew up in a gentle, simple day. We could leave our doors unlocked at night when we went to church, for nobody ever molested the premises. Today no decent woman walks the street at night and I dare not walk in city parks in the day. Last week a maintenance man added a chain lock to my motel room, already fitted with bolts and keys. Nothing is safe from the thieves and vandals. Innocent people are murdered by perverts and demonized denizens of darkness. The newsstands and bookracks reek with putridity. Society stinks to high heaven.

I titled this book, *I Walk Through the Valley*. Thank God, I'm walking THROUGH it. Beyond this Valley lies home. For me there is no home down here. There is an apartment but it is vacant with no one to greet me when I return. There are relatives and friends who have been wonderful but there is no home. Paul had a desire to depart and be with Christ but was willing to remain in the flesh awhile if necessary. That is where I stand exactly. There is nothing morbid about wanting to go to heaven. It is the weary pilgrim anxious to get through the Valley and safe to the other side. My dearest is already home and where she is I want to be. This morning finds me in a motel room in a strange city and what can be more bleak! But I think of those voyagers to Rome who ". . . about midnight . . . deemed that they drew near to some country" (Acts 27:27). I am nearing another land and I'm homesick for it.

Meanwhile I am "homed in God." "Lord, Thou hast been our dwelling place in all generations" (Psalms 90:1). ". . . your life is hid with Christ in God" (Colossians 3:3). In my heart I am already home! I am a citizen of a land I have never seen. I became a citizen of that other world when I trusted Christ as my Saviour. It is now a spiritual Kingdom but when I depart from here I join a heavenly throng awaiting the resurrection and a millennium on this earth when Jesus takes over. After that comes eternity, new heavens, and a new earth. What a prospect! But to be in Christ is to be home. My home is a Person and it will one day be a place.

But I am lonesome today. I want to go home for I don't belong here. "This world is not my home, I'm only passing through." How many times a day do I find myself asking, "Dear, how is it over there?" I can almost hear her sing in the kitchen as I used to hear her. She's home. And I'm a day nearer than I was yesterday.

42
I Trust in God—But Why?

I am now in Texas and that Texas wind blows all day long.
There is abundant walking space and this morning I got out
early. The October weather has been glorious and I must make
the most of it before a "Norther" blows in.

On my desk is a picture of Sara that I treasure above all
others. It is not a formal dressed-up picture of which I have
many. It is a snapshot taken on the Blue Ridge Parkway last
summer on our last visit to that favored spot. She wore a plain
little pink dress and she stood at a lookout that commands a
breathtaking view of the valley below. It wasn't overposed and
she looks as though she might speak. The original was a tiny
negative and was taken on a cheap little camera. We sent the
print to Eastman Kodak and they enlarged it into a thing of
beauty. I carry it in a double frame and on the opposite side
of the frame facing the picture is that precious poem that
begins, "Should you go first, and I remain. . . ."

On my lonely walk this morning I realized afresh that God
has shut me up to Himself and Himself alone. There is no one
else to whom I can turn. There are friends and relatives but
the other half of my life is gone. God is my portion and my
reward. I know not what to do but my eyes are upon Him. But
I must be sure that I look to Him in truth and trust and love
and not merely because I must and there is nothing else that

I can do. There is not much to be gained from dependence on God simply as a last resort. If I go around looking for some broken reed, some arm of the flesh on which to lean, then I have not learned my lesson and God must deal further with me. He does not come to our relief until we stop trying to save ourselves. Sometimes a lifeguard must knock out a drowning man because in his desperation that man might hold on so tightly that both might drown. When we reach utter desperation and are satisfied with God alone, then He may step in with help we never dreamed of and never could have found. To pretend that we are marooned on God and at the same time make clever plans to meet our own needs is hypocrisy.

Throughout the Old Testament God reproved His people for seeking security by making alliances with other nations. He would have them look to Him alone. God promised Abraham a son in his old age but when Sarah and Abraham took matters in their own hands and brought Hagar and Ishmael into the picture, trouble began that continues to this day. When we stand utterly committed to God He will work out the details of whatever plans He may have for our future. We are to cooperate with Him in those plans when He begins to reveal them, but that is different from drawing up our own plans and asking Him to bless them.

Psalm 123 is the prayer of a man shut up to God: "Behold, as the eyes of servants look unto the hand of their masters, and the eyes of a maiden unto the hand of her mistress; so our eyes wait upon the Lord our God, until that he have mercy upon us." The New Testament calls it "looking unto Jesus" *(see* Hebrews 12:2). When we reach that blessed point we may rest in peace for God will not fail us. He may test our faith and try our patience but He will perfect that which concerns us.

I trust in God—but why? Because there is nothing else I can do or because I love Him for Himself?

43
The Picture on the Desk

I have read of a man who lived beside a river. He was not interested in the people who lived on the other side until his daughter went over there to live. After that he developed a great interest in those people. Every time I look at the picture of my Sara standing by the overlook in the mountains I take fresh interest in the next world. She is now a citizen no longer of this earth but of the land where the spirits of the saints enjoy the presence of God. I never have been so interested in heaven as now. My dear one belongs to another country and not only she but a dear father and mother and many dear ones of other days. The population has shifted and the old crowd I started with is just about gone. I'm one of the last leaves on the tree and the wind blows hard.

I find myself calling to my sweetheart, "Honey, how is it

over there?" I'd give a lot to know. Does she know what goes
on here? As one of the cloud of witnesses I think she does. I
do know that now I have a feeling about it all that I never had
before, for the one I knew and loved for thirty-three years is
now on an entirely different status and is part of that land of
mystery. My Lord has told me enough about it to fill me with
an unutterable longing to find out more and I can hardly wait
to begin. He has been a citizen of both worlds and has told us
all we can stand to know down here. Either I believe He was
the Son of God who came to tell me of that fair world and how
to get there, or I am lost in a world of conjecture and despair.
I stake everything on Him, who He is and what He did and
does.

So when I look at the dear picture on my desk I am not
merely refreshing my memory of one loved and gone. I am
looking at one who still lives but has changed her residence.
She is now in the dwelling place Her Saviour prepared for her.
Mine is waiting for later occupancy. We used to talk about the
time our Social Security would start. It starts for me tomorrow
but she won't need hers for now she is enjoying a new installment of Eternal Security. It began when she trusted her Saviour and the presence of the Holy Spirit in her heart was the
first down payment. "Blessed assurance, Jesus is mine! Oh,
what a foretaste of glory divine!"

Tomorrow I can draw my Social Security, no matter how
much I earn otherwise. But I have a heavenly income this
world knows nothing about. Sara has entered into fullest enjoyment of hers. I greet her across the great divide and long to
join her. We used to talk about retirement homes and where

we might go. God has looked after all that hereafter and we shall not retire but serve Him forever.

I get excited about it. The picture does not sadden me with memories of things we can never do again down here. It thrills me with prospects of what we shall do forever beginning pretty soon. Some of it may begin right here when my Lord reigns over a redeemed earth with His saints. Who knows but we may stand again on that same mountain lookout when the restitution of all things and the redemption of creation come to pass!

44
The Little Christmas Tree

Today at an autograph party, I browsed in one of my old books, *Rest for the Weary*, written many years ago. There is a piece in it about our little Christmas tree. At a Christmas supper one evening long past, this tiny ornament on the table appealed to us so much that Sara and I brought it home. It was a fragile little wisp of a tree even then, so dainty that we handled it with tenderest care. It has been on the table in our dining nook every Christmas. In my book I wrote: "As the years lengthen behind us, we are more inclined now to wonder how many more times this blessed season will find us here."

Well, it won't be long until they'll be singing "It's Beginning to Look a Lot Like Christmas" but the blessed season won't find US here. All that is left is the little tree and me. One day after Sara left for heaven I got the precious momento out and it still stands bravely though stooped with age. The tiny tinsel angel on it is bowed and not so bright. We're somewhat alike, I'm afraid, but come Christmas I'm going to set it on the table again. There'll be a vacant chair across from me for it will be Sara's first Christmas in heaven. But the little tree and I will muster all the courage possible and with my creaky old voice I might even try a verse of "Joy To The World." For though the heart aches and the voice shakes and tears fill the eyes, I'm still all for Christmas and all it truly means. For I am celebrating the coming to this earth of One who mastered death and the grave and who assures me of a glad reunion with those we have loved long since and lost awhile. I'm rejoicing in the coronation of the dearest one I've known, promotion from pain and grief to the courts of heaven. I'm not hiding the little tree among my souvenirs as a sad reminder of days forever past. As long as it can stand I'll set it up as a symbol of victory ahead.

Run up your flag, my dear sorrowing one, and wave your banner! If your life is hid with Christ in God together with your loved one, it matters not on which side of death you stand, you are both somewhere and God has bound Himself by His word to bring you together again. Don't become the victim of tender memories or worship at their shrine, but let them whet your expectation for better times ahead. ". . . because I live, ye shall live also" (John 14:19). "I will come again and receive you unto myself" (14:3). And with Him will be those who reached the Father's house ahead of us. We shall be raised together with them who are asleep in Jesus to meet the Lord in the air AND SO SHALL WE EVER BE WITH THE LORD. What a day, what a day that will be!

If anybody sees me, come Christmas, at my table with the little Christmas tree, he might see mixed emotions. But there'll be a song in my heart for I'm getting ready to move from that little tree to the tree of life beside the river, that tree whose leaves mean healing forever for the aches and pains of hurting hearts down here. I keep my little tree here as a reminder of days when times were better. I'd like to set it up over there as a symbol of days when times were worse just before they turned bright forever!

45
Encompassed

It has been said that people who are living in the sunshine MAY believe but we who are in the shadows MUST. Like Peter we would say, "To whom shall we go?" Where else can we turn? That is the poorest reason for being a Christian but it will do to start with. There are better reasons, as Peter went on to say, but we can begin with the matter of alternatives.

There are mysteries galore and much that we cannot under-stand, but look up any other road and there is only despair.

But it is not enough to say, "This or else." As a man thinketh in his heart so is he, and we are bidden to think on whatsoever things are true, honest, just, pure, lovely, and of good report. Think faith and faith will grow. Think doubt and doubt will grow. Whatever you feed and exercise will grow. It is not mere autosuggestion, it just works that way. Fear and unbelief and depression gain strength as we give them expression in thought or in word. On the other hand, if we accept the Word of God, assert it and act upon it, then faith grows strong while doubt shrinks and shrivels. We often have to do it in spite of feelings and circumstances when not only feelings but facts make light of our faith, but there is a higher set of facts than what we see and feel when we look not at the temporal but at the eternal.

If we believe what God has said we cannot wish our dear ones back in the misery of this vale of tears. How selfish of me to pine because Sara is not here when I remember where she IS! When I remember the months of pain and grief and dark-ness she endured, how glad I am to know that now she enjoys bliss utterly beyond anything my poor mind can fathom! Every pleasure she ever knew in this poor world cannot equal one moment of heaven. I will plod along until I overtake her but, Lord, let me never be so foolish as to wish she were back in a place like this!

It is my intention to preach victory and not defeat. A few days ago I preached to a host of young preachers in a great theological seminary. They applauded me and gave me a stand-ing ovation at the finish. They did not go out with drooping heads and doubting hearts. I preached what I knew to be true, feel like it or not, and God blessed it. My mind is made up.

I am imprisoned in a motel room in East Texas. I rode for five hours in the rain to get here and it has rained ever since with not a glimpse of sunshine. I'm not whistling my way past the graveyard. The poor disfigured body of my dear one lies there but her spirit awaits a new heavenly form lovely beyond compare. As much as I miss her, I am glad that now she belongs to that cloud of witnesses that hold us in full survey.

A dear old preacher labored late one night on a sermon to be given next day to a handful of parishioners. His wife said, "Dear, why do you work so hard on your message? Only a few will hear it."

"You forget, my dear," he replied, "how large my audience will be!"

Nothing is trivial here if heaven looks on. We shall play a better game if, "seeing we are encompassed," we remember who is in the grandstand!

46
If Only I Had. . . .

A book given to me by a Christian friend has a fine paragraph titled, "If Only I Had. . . ." It deals with regrets and self-accusation after our loved ones are gone, bemoaning what we failed to do, blaming ourselves for what we might have done and didn't. Such worry eats like a cancer and will drive us to distraction if we allow it.

After my dear one was gone, I mulled over how I might have changed things and how her life might have been saved. At the outset of her illness I was away preaching and in her letters she did not let me know the full extent of her decline. She did not want to frighten me or shorten my meetings. If I had known what her real trouble was, I would have taken her to a famous clinic at the very beginning. There were other delays and mistakes we might have remedied although we thought we were doing the right thing at the time. All these regrets plagued me and I had to learn to close the door on them. The past is past and forgetting the things which are behind is an everlasting must if we are to survive.

To be sure, if we do wrong knowingly we ought to confess it and claim the cleansing blood and God's forgiveness. We are to learn whatever lessons are to be gained from our mistakes. But nothing is gained by wallowing in morbid self-condemnation.

> If ye have taken a step aside,
> Some hap mistaken o'ertaken you,
> Yet still keep up a decent pride
> And don't o'er far demean ye.

It does no good to continually accuse and condemn ourselves. Things might even have been worse if we had done some things we think would have been better. Let us put the past, good and bad, and whatever might have been into God's hands and resume our pilgrimage.

Martha complained when Jesus finally reached Bethany after the death of Lazarus, "Lord, if thou hadst been here, my brother had not died" (John 11:21). But a greater miracle was awaiting them than could have been wrought if Jesus had come sooner. "IF only I had. . . ." is no fit lament when it is too late and "IF only you had. . . ." is no fit way to pray. God makes no mistakes at all and our mistakes, if mistakes they were, can be left in the hands of Him who makes all things work together for good to His own.

We need to find that "Land of Beginning Again" so beautifully set forth in the precious poem, the land where all our mistakes can be left like a ragged old cloak at the door and never put on again. It is false penance to stew in bitter regret. Those we might have helped better understand it all now and God our Father forgives us. It is Satan's clever device to wear us down in wretched self-rebuke though it may look pious enough in the sackcloth of remorse.

There is not time to waste in moaning, "If only I had . . . ." There are better things to do.

47
The Eternal Contemporary

When Moses asked, "What shall I say when the children of Israel want to know in what name I come?" God answered, "I AM THAT I AM. Tell them I AM hath sent me unto you" *(see* Exodus 3:14). Jesus said, "Before Abraham was, I am" (John 8:58).

God lives in the Eternal Now. Jesus Christ is the same yesterday AND TODAY and forever. With Him there is no past and future. He is the eternal Contemporary. We do not serve a dead leader like Mohammed or Buddha. We do not dwell in a musty past and spend our time maintaining shrines and worn-out traditions. We are not the custodians of a museum, dusting relics and archives of a day forever past. We are citizens of an Eternal Today.

The church has spent too much time propping up the past and predicting the future. It is all one piece. We need not worry for fear the faith of our fathers will have no relevance today. Times have changed, they tell us, but time makes no difference to the great I AM. He outlasts all our little systems; they have their day and cease to be. With Him a thousand years are as a day and a day as a thousand years. It would be amusing if it were not so pathetic, the concern of those who are afraid the Gospel will be out of date. It is never out of date for it is dateless, it bears the postmark of no age or time. "The old-time religion" is a misnomer for it is not merely old-time but new-time, any-time, all-the-time. God is not running an antique shop. Behold, He makes all things new! The Christian is dateless and in the little calendars of men He never belongs with the files of yesterday.

There is only one thing that Jesus WAS in time and one place where He WAS and is not now. He said, "I am He that liveth, and was dead" (Revelation 1:18). He died unto sin once. He is not dead now. He was in a grave once but He is not there now. He died that we might say one day, "I, too, WAS dead but now I live forevermore." We wonder about death, we ask countless questions, we speculate and surmise. One thing ought to satisfy us forever—Jesus Christ WAS dead. He explored that world and came back, the first of a new race of those who may die but do not stay dead. He has the keys of hell and death. He mastered those realms and we stand in His triumph. We ought to stop shaking our heads when God's people depart from this earth and their bodies cease to function. To hear some of these mourners, one would think that the saints disappear forever. The very worst of it is only a temporary interval while bodies return to dust, but do not look for those departed ones in mausoleums or under ten feet of earth. Thank God, my Lord died too but He died to make death a WAS, the last enemy to go.

"I was dead but I am alive forevermore." Get contemporary, brother, in the Everlasting NOW! We are not victims of time but victors of eternity! Let us go forth in the name of our Lord and when the world asks for our credentials, let us say, "I AM hath sent me. I do not represent what merely WAS or WILL BE but Him who forever IS."

48
A Day in October

October was never lovelier than today. I have been to my beloved Carolina mountains with dear ones, Sara's brother and sister and two sisters-in-law. I have often said that when I married Sara I got a great bargain, for along with a marvelous wife I got a wonderful family. Nobody on earth could have been more gracious and helpful during these sad months than the entire Allred clan.

But today a fair face was absent and a dear voice silent. I found myself looking at the mountains Sara and I loved so much, humming some old love songs of long ago like "I'm Lonesome For You, That's All" and "Somewhere A Voice Is Calling." They say that time heals all wounds but time moves slowly and the wound is deep. They say you never get over it, you just learn to live with it.

But everything is not on the debit side of this ledger. There is gain as well as loss. My Heavenly Father has been good to me. Before Sara became ill I was so tired and needed rest so much that the doctor urged me to lighten my load. Then came five months of deepest trial as we fought a losing battle with an awful disease. Yet God gave strength to see it through even to hold her hand in the last few days when life had really departed save for a heart kept going by a machine. There was grace for the funeral and the days of getting business details straightened out and a new adjustment to a lonely life. There was sleep provided by Him who keepeth Israel and who Himself never slumbers. It has been next to miraculous. And I have been deluged with calls and cards and letters and gifts and countless gracious ministrations from a host of God's people all over America. Above all, there has been a new sense of God's presence and promise and provision beyond any words to record. I can sing "My Heavenly Father Watches Over Me" with a meaning it never had for me before.

There has been profound human grief of which I am not ashamed. I would be ashamed if I didn't have it. There have been tears aplenty but I am assured that one day God Himself will wipe them all away. They are preserved in His bottle and recorded in His Book *(see* Psalms 56:8). But there has been joy unspeakable and full of glory as we trust Him "though now we see Him not, yet believing" *(see* 1 Peter 1:8).

Tonight I sit in this lonely apartment. I would give just about everything if we could sit once more and enjoy a favorite television program. Things once taken for granted loom large now. I would say to every husband and wife, "Count no day unimportant if you still have each other, for the day will come when you would give everything for just one day, any ordinary day, you once shared together."

But do not despair if you walk alone. God will make up your loss and give you beauty for ashes, the oil of joy for mourning, the garment of praise for the spirit of heaviness." He will not leave you comfortless, orphaned in the storm. I never felt more like an orphan—like a motherless child, as the old spiritual puts it—but I have His Word and He has already proven it in numberless ways. My loss is but temporary for I journey toward a glad reunion. My gain is eternal for until I regain my dear

one later, I am blessed with countless compensations to tide me
over until we meet again.

49
As a Little Child

I have been listening to one of the very brilliant men of our
day being interviewed on television. His wealth of knowledge
is enviable, his language flawless. He ventured a few remarks
about life to come and indicated that he neither knew nor
cared much about it but suggested that there might be some
sort of immortality, that this might not be the last of us. He
quoted a saying to the effect that hunger for food presupposes
bread.

His listeners seemed charmed but I was reminded of a lady
who listened recently to a lecture that said nothing for one
hour. When the speaker finished, she gurgled to the man next
to her, "Wasn't it marvelous!" and when he replied that he
really didn't say anything, she replied, "But he intimated so
much!"

". . . the natural man receiveth not the things of the Spirit
of God: for they are foolishness unto him: neither can he know
them, because they are spiritually discerned" (1 Corinthians
2:14). That explains why this sage on television said so little

about so much. He would probably view with lofty disdain some humble soul reading his Bible and believing every word of its grand and glorious message about the world to come. Alas for a keen mind that has not learned "that truth to flesh and sense unknown, that life is ever lord of death and love can never lose its own." Even that does not say enough, but it does say something.

I have come to the sunset slope and through a summer of grief with all my hopes pinned on One who came to this poor earth long ago to clear up the mystery and heal the misery. I have walked beside the Sea of Galilee and meditated on the Mount of Olives and thanked my God that on those sacred spots stood God Himself made flesh and spent a few precious years with us down here. If He were not God made flesh He would be history's greatest impostor for He claimed no less than that. He met and mastered our problem—sin—and answered our longing for a life beyond. But the secret has been kept from the wise and prudent and revealed unto babes. An astute philosopher can never grasp it by sheer intellect. His Ph.D. gives him no instrument for discerning it. It pours contempt on all his pride. It is "the foolishness of God," moronic to the natural man but manna from heaven to the humble heart.

The doors of the Kingdom of heaven are open to all who have the twin keys—conversion and childlikeness *(see* Matthew 18:3). Our Lord spoke of children, the childish *(see* Matthew 11:16,17), and the childlike. Revival comes to the church when its members cease being childish—babes who won't grow up—and become childlike. Christians begin a new day in their lives when they make the same change. And the sinner must come in the same lowly gate to become a child of God.

The smart intellect I heard on television can enter the Kingdom but he will have to come just like the rest of us, not headfirst but heartfirst. They are not the same. Only cabbage has head and heart in the same place.

If Jesus appeared on television today He would not present some shrewd philosopher as His model. He would still address us with a little child upon His knee. For of such is the Kingdom of heaven.

50
Waiting

I am waiting in a Texas airport. I missed my connection, so here I sit like a bird in the wilderness waiting for a later plane. I've had a poor excuse for a lunch, the best I could get, and I can only mark time. Life's unavoidable delays and disappointments are part of it and we had better learn early that things just don't run along like we plan them in this rickety old world. Pity the perfectionist who takes great pains and gives them to others when his little schedule is disrupted.

I'm not feeling well and if ever I wanted to get home—not home really, just Greensboro, for what made it home is no longer there—it was today. I'm getting used to things not working out in apple-pie order. I'm glad there is a destiny that shapes our ends, rough-hew them as we may. The best we can do with anything is to approximate with a reasonable facsimile of what we really wanted to be and do. I believe God will perfect that which concerns us, give it form and symmetry. We are complete in Him and when we stand before the throne in Him complete we shall discover that all the while, His fullness flowed around our incompleteness, round our restlessness His rest.

An awful lot of waiting is in order in this old world. Other things besides coffee need time to percolate. Our fondest dreams and loftiest aspirations lose much luster by the time they have run through the sieve of our faulty minds and awkward speech. Sometimes the finished product bears little resemblance to the ideal we started with. The best of God's saints fall far short of Christlikeness. Too much of old Adam gets mixed up in the process and the flesh often spoils the work of the Spirit. We get in a hurry to tear open the cocoon and release the butterfly. Our clumsy hands wreck God's delicate timing.

I found the loss of my airplane connection exasperating. I finally got myself settled down and decided to save time and shoe leather instead of prancing all over the place. If it does you no good as you read this, it has at least helped me. I do a lot of preaching to myself. The doctor often needs some of his own medicine. Wishing has its place and working is ever commendable but waiting also has its rewards.

And now the wait is over and I'm flying over Atlanta in lovely October sunshine. And when life's long wait is over, may

I head for home singing, "Sun, moon and stars forgot, Upward
I fly." Or maybe He will come first and we who remain shall
be caught up together with the risen dear ones to meet the
Lord in the air. Then the wait that seems so long just now will
be forgotten when TOMORROW becomes an eternal TO-
DAY!

> The strife will not be long;
> This day the noise of battle,
> The next, the victor's song.
> >   GEORGE DUFFIELD

Postscript
Threescore and Twelve

I am writing this on my seventy-second birthday. God has
given me the Scriptural threescore and ten and added two
more. 1973 has been the darkest and saddest year of my life
Beginning in April I have walked through the Valley to this
hour. My dearest left on September 2 for the other world and
I am left without my helpmeet in my declining years and in
one of the bleakest periods of national and world history.

But 1973 has not been without compensation. I have been

brought to a new dependence on God Himself, able to sing, "Now Thee alone I seek, give what is best." I have been made aware of a multitude of friends whose love and prayers and assistance in every way has lightened my load and brightened my road. God opens more doors than I can enter and each day I draw nearer to glad reunion.

"I have been young, and now am old; yet have I not seen the righteous forsaken, nor his seed begging bread" (Psalms 37:25). Our Lord asked His disciples, "When I sent you . . . lacked ye anything? And they said, Nothing" (Luke 22:35). There has always been enough and there always will be to do all that He wants me to do as long as He wants me to do it.

I have not been able in all these years to report dramatic subjective experiences. There was a time when I read of such and sought to duplicate them. I have heard many accounts of visions and revelations, stories of men and women being mightily empowered, invaded with peace and joy and energy for body, mind, and spirit. I sought such rare moments but cannot relate anything sensational. I find my prayer best summed up in the old hymn:

> I ask no dream, no prophet ecstasies,
> No sudden rending of the veil of clay,
> No angel visitant, no opening skies;
> But take the dimness of my soul away.
> GEORGE CROLY

With me it has simply been TRUST AND OBEY. I have had high moments and blessed intervals but trying to live on occasional trips to the third heaven makes a hectic life and Paul himself had to find that it is far better to learn that God's grace is sufficient and His strength is made perfect in our weakness.

> All the way my Saviour leads me,
> What have I to ask beside?
> Can I doubt His tender mercy,
> Who thro' life has been my Guide?
>
> FANNY J. CROSBY

****

I write these final lines in lovely St. Augustine, Florida. Once again, God has brought His tired servant to the right place at the right time. This morning I watched a glorious sunrise. The place where I stay faces the waterfront and I stroll along the promenade looking across the bay to the whitecaps on the ocean beach beyond.

It was in Florida that I met Sara and fell in love with her. I remember that during our courtship I went away on a preaching engagement, and when I returned she met me at the railroad station in her radiant loveliness. That was the first of countless times she met me for thirty-three years when I returned home tired from my preaching journeys.

I have but one request, My Father. When I reach that distant shore, I can wait to see the pearly gates, the golden streets, and the many mansions. But grant, dear God, that after I have first seen Him, whom having not seen I love, my dearest may be next to meet me, just like she used to do.